Starting, MANAGING, and Promoting the SMALL LIBRARY

Starting, MANAGING, and Promoting the SMALL LIBRARY

Robert A. Berk

M. E. Sharpe, Inc.
Armonk, New York
London, England

Available in the United Kingdom and Europe from M. E. Sharpe,
Publishers, 3 Henrietta Street, London WC2E 8LU.

Library of Congress Cataloging-in-Publication Data

Berk, Robert A.
　　Starting, managing, and promoting the small library / by Robert
Berk.
　　　　p.　　cm.
　　Includes bibliographical references.
　　ISBN 0-87332-576-1
　　1. Small libraries—Administration. 2. Small libraries—Collection
development. I. Title.
Z678.B48　　1989　　　　　　　　　　　　　　　　　89-10704
025.1—dc20　　　　　　　　　　　　　　　　　　　　　CIP

Printed in the United States of America

∞

BB　10　9　8　7　6　5　4　3　2　1

For Laura, Holly, and Erika,
along with all my former students in librarianship.

Contents

Acknowledgments

As author I am solely responsible for content, but it was only through the consistent support of my longtime friend and colleague, Dr. Donald D. Foos, that this work has finally been completed. Special thanks go to Sue Ealy for her multiple keyboarding efforts and to Roger Guard and Joe Profaizer for arriving in time.

Introduction

This book is intended to serve as an introductory work on how to initiate and run a very small library. Its emphasis is on the one-person library, most commonly referred to as a special library, and as such is designed to aid the individual without library training who is suddenly faced with the need to plan and organize a library. A special library is one that is intended to meet the information needs of a business, or of a special group of users with clearly defined subject interests such as musicians, lawyers, physicians, and business people. Similar management problems are also associated with the very small public library, and issues addressed here should be of interest to those librarians as well. Further, it is the author's hope that the book will prove useful to librarians already involved in the operation of very small libraries by providing a means of review, and by identifying forgotten or new concepts and practices. Finally, library schools offering courses in special, public, and school librarianship should find this work useful.

The book is arranged to lead the user from the establishment of the library through the acquisition of materials, their organization, and the use of the library's collection in providing services to meet a variety of information needs. Other chapters deal with more effective management of the library through automation, evaluation of services, arrangement of physical facilities, effective public relations, and cooperation with other information agencies. The importance of conserving the librarian's time is emphasized throughout the work. With a limited staff, time is the key to productivity, and any savings in time enables the librarian to provide better and more effective means of meeting users' information needs.

Few references are included in the body of the work, but each chapter has a list of recommended readings. Older literature, when useful, has intentionally been included because its continuing value is often overlooked.

Starting, MANAGING, and Promoting the SMALL LIBRARY

1 Starting a Library

One of the major functions of the librarian who is planning to bring library service to a group of potential users is to secure support for the concept of library service. Achieving this support for a proposed library, especially a very small one, may be difficult because the lack of library personnel will limit the extent to which reference service can be planned for the new facility. Support for a proposed library must first come from the top management of the business, organization, or institution in which the library is to function and whose goals the library will attempt to achieve. However, it is unlikely that everyone in the higher decision-making positions of the organization will see the need for the creation of a library. The attitude encountered may be, "We haven't had a library up until now and we have done very well without one." Even a one-person library that is capable of providing well-designed information services is an expensive undertaking if it is to be done right, and the would-be librarian may have a hard time convincing a reluctant manager that such a capital outlay is really in the best interests of the organization. Since creation of the library may well be dependent upon overcoming resistance, developing strategies aimed at convincing management of the need for library services is the responsibility of the librarian.

Demonstrating a need for library service

A number of arguments favor the establishment of library services for virtually any type of modern day endeavor. An unemployed librarian might start by trying to convince the top management of a local company that a library is needed if that company is to prosper, with the desired outcome being that the librarian would be hired to create that library and to begin meeting the information needs of the organization's employees. A useful strategy in this instance would be to document the number of firms or organizations with similar interests who have already established library services. The hardest fact to demonstrate, but undoubtedly the most relevant, is how the establishment of a library will aid in the attainment of organizational goals. In the business world it is necessary to demonstrate how library services influence organizational profits. Although profit is not important to all types of small libraries, in organizations where profits are important, everything, including the provision of library services, must be viewed relative to this goal. Directories such as the one by Darnay for special libraries and information centers may be useful for gaining a picture of current library development in a given area of specialization as well as for providing a wealth of additional information.

A potentially strong means for demonstrating the need for library service would be to show past situations in which information needs went unmet and how these unmet needs adversely affected the attainment of the organization's goals. Perhaps a contract was lost because of a bid that was too high based on   lack of information or the use of inaccurate information. An examination of the company's internal documents and interviews with key personnel may identify such incidents. If adverse situations can be identified, it becomes the job of the librarian to suggest how a library might have overcome such critical incidents by providing information in an accurate and timely fashion.

Another important role for the librarian to play in promoting the establishment of a library is that of change agent. A change agent is one who plans an active campaign to persuade others to accept an idea or product, or to begin using certain products or services. Some change agents may only provide pertinent information while others actually perform demonstrations and offer trial uses, but the end goal of every change agent's efforts is the adoption or use of a particular product, service, or idea. All individuals in sales are change agents, and this is exactly what the individual hoping to establish a library must be. In order to do so, the librarian must first demonstrate a thorough knowledge of what is needed. By talking with individuals on a one-to-one basis, the librarian can begin to gain support for the library concept.

Individuals in key positions within the organization must be identified for the change agent's campaign. Those in charge of personnel, those in positions where long-range planning is most important, and those in roles where budgeting and other organizational decisions are made are potential heavy users of library services. The librarian should concentrate on persuading people in these and similar positions. Some of those targeted might include the president of the organization, the vice-president, head of research and development, head of marketing, head of personnel, and head of laboratory facilities.

The librarian may not be able to garner much of the valuable time of these people, so face-to-face contacts may be limited to only one or two visits. The librarian must be well prepared to make both formal and informal presentations, often with little advance warning, in order to convince such individuals that library services are well worth their consideration. Larger formal presentations may be useful when they are made to decision makers, but the interaction of the librarian as a change agent on a one-to-one basis will usually provide the answers to individual questions and be most instrumental in persuading key staff members to accept the proposed library.

With the support of top management and other key decision makers within the organization, the result is likely to be "go ahead." Ideally, this will lead to the employment of the change agent as the new company librarian.

Identifying users' needs

It is possible, but certainly not preferable, for the librarian to remain isolated while planning information services. A better approach is to actively involve potential users in planning for information services that will be most appropriate in meeting their individual needs. Once library services become available, potential users must be encouraged to use these services. This may be difficult if users have had no say about the services to be offered.

Hierarchically speaking, the universe of information services consists of all potential information sources and services, all potential information sources and services that the user is aware of, all sources and services to which the user has access, and all sources and services that the user actually uses. Each of the lower levels is a subset of the level above it. It is true that many individuals really have little idea of what services are available or possible. Because of this, one might decide to exclude potential users from the planning process. This would be a mistake, because even if their knowledge is limited in this area, their involvement provides the librarian with an opportunity to expand their awareness of information products and services.

The process used to determine what sources and services potential users of the library are already aware of, which ones they currently utilize, and which others they would like to see included in their library is called a user study. It is the responsibility of the librarian to be aware of the existence of all potentially useful sources and services. This knowledge can be used to provide a "shopping list" of available sources and services as part of the user study to aid potential users in their selection. How can the librarian become familiar with all of the potentially useful sources and services? This is part of the basic education for librarianship, and a variety of sources can be used in compiling the shopping list. Vendors of bibliographic search services publish reference manuals and newsletters detailing system capabilities, database availability, etc. DIALOG Information Services, for example, publishes *Chronolog* and BRS Information Technologies issues a *Bulletin*. Both are monthly newsletters designed to keep librarians informed. Library journals for each special field will provide information on services being developed and tested by other librarians serving similar user groups. For example, the *Bulletin of the Medical Library Association* will aid hospital librarians, the *Law Library Journal* legal librarians, the *American Theological Library Association Newsletter* theological librarians, the *Music Library Association Newsletter* music librarians, and so on. Specialized library publications provide insights into sources and services that might be adapted to any small library. One should become familiar with titles such as *Special Libraries, Advanced Technologies/ Libraries, Database, Library Hi Tech, Online, The Reference Librarian, RQ,* and *Science & Technology Libraries,* to name a few.

Other sources of information might include various literature guides and monographs describing information sources and services for a particular field or for special or small libraries in general. Roper's *Introduction to Reference Sources in the Health Sciences* is helpful for health sciences librarians as are the volumes of the latest edition of the *Handbook of Medical Library Practice*, the monograph on *Hospital Library Management*, and the British work, *Hospital Libraries and Work with Disabled in the Community*. General works to consult would include *Special Libraries: A Guide for Management* published by the Special Libraries Association, the Jackson compilation of published readings on special librarianship, the Aluri and Robinson *Guide to U.S. Government Scientific and Technical Resources*, and Subramanyam's *Scientific and Technical Information Resources*. Lancaster's *Measurement and Evaluation of Library Services* includes a chapter entitled "The range and scope of library services" that could also prove useful.

Librarians should be alert to specific user needs that might trigger the development of a new or previously unused information source or service. Many information services have been designed because an imaginative librarian was faced with the need to provide information different from or in a manner not found in library literature. Traditional sources and services will continue to be used, but advances in technology and a critical examination of existing ways by which information is provided may lead to the development of approaches as yet not imagined. Listening to users discuss what would be most desirable may lead the librarian to paths of innovation. Please refer to the end of this chapter for a list of sources and services that might appear as part of a shopping list within a user study.

Conducting the user study

The methodology for the user study must secure the needed information from the library's potential users. The determining factor for the technique to be used is usually the size of the potential user group. The best means of gathering this information is probably by interviewing individuals using a checklist to ensure that the same information is gathered from each person. The interview process provides the librarian with an opportunity to interact with each potential user, clarify responses, and begin a personal public relations campaign for the library. The marketing of library services can actually begin during the user study when the interview method is employed. Unfortunately, the interview process requires the most time on the part of both the librarian and the individuals being interviewed. This method is only feasible in a very small library with a limited number of interviews to be held. In larger libraries, the interviewing may be divided among several individuals. Interview questions will usually be very similar to those one would use in a printed questionnaire. The advantage of the interview is the ability to expand on a stated question by means of probes to elicit additional detailed information. This enriches the data available for planning. The format for an abbreviated interview schedule might appear as follows:

1. In which department of the company do you work?
2. What types of information needs do you encounter in your daily work?
Probe: Explain current, everyday, and exhaustive needs to the user and record all that are appropriate for this individual.
Probe: Attempt to determine the frequency with which these needs occur.
3. Do you have occasion to use foreign language materials in connection with your work?
Probe: If yes, which languages are consulted most often?
Probe: Would translations be more useful than foreign language materials?
Probe: What problems are presented when using foreign language materials?
(Interviewer: Write a brief summary of the respondent's comments regarding the importance of foreign language materials for the development of new products for the company.)
4. How do you attempt to meet your information needs currently?
Probe: Distinguish different sources used for the current, everyday, and exhaustive approaches.
Probe: How often do you seek out a colleague for a face-to-face consultation relative to an information need?
Probe: When this approach is employed, how much of your time does it entail?

This list of questions can be expanded until the interviewer has gained all of the information needed for effective planning of in-

STARTING A LIBRARY 9

formation services. The degree to which probes are employed and the amount of data derived will vary from interview to interview, but each individual will be asked the same basic questions. In almost any setting, if the group to be interviewed exceeds fifty, some other method of gathering information should be considered because of the time and expense that are involved.

The distribution of written questionnaires can be effective when surveying larger potential user populations. One problem with this is that the number of questionnaires that are actually completed and returned may not be large enough to give a true representation of the information needs of the potential user group. One would hope for a return rate of least 75 percent with representation from all types of potential users as a means of providing some degree of confidence in the planning data. Questionnaire distribution is a "one shot" approach, and care must be taken in advance to ensure that questions are clear and that they will be interpreted in the same fashion by each of the respondents. Therefore, it is extremely important that the questionnaire be pretested on a few individuals who are representative of the entire group so that any problems may be corrected before the final distribution. The pretest should be repeated each time questions are changed.

One important means of ensuring that individuals who receive the questionnaire actually respond to the questions and return their answers is to provide a cover letter explaining the purpose of the questionnaire and the deadline for its return. It may be highly useful to have the cover letter carry the signature of the president of the organization or institution or some other person whose importance and authority will underscore the need to respond. Please refer to the end of this chapter for an abbreviated questionnaire format for a user study.

Other ways of obtaining information about potential users and their information needs include diary studies and the content analysis of library or other records. Both of these methods are more suitable in a situation where a library already exists, but for one reason or another there is a need to re-examine its services. A useful discussion of user study methodology is offered by Bare.

Regardless of the methodology employed for the user study, data are needed to respond to the following questions:

What types of work are company personnel engaged in?
What information needs are associated with this work?

How do those with information needs go about meeting these needs?

How successful are their efforts?

What services should the library provide?

If the user study is successful, the librarian should then be ready to make some decisions relating to the creation of services to be offered by the library. Information from the user study will enable the librarian to determine (1) what types of materials to place in the collection; (2) how recent these materials should be, whether older material should be retained, and if so, for how long; (3) how much floor space will be required for the library; (4) what seating and study arrangements will be needed; (5) what equipment and supplies will be required; (6) what information services should the library provide and what services should be contracted for; (7) what types of cooperative agreements should be made with other libraries and providers of information; and the most important question of all, (8) how can the library best aid the organization in the attainment of its goals?

It should now be apparent that a library, even a very small one, will not appear in an organization by spontaneous generation. However, if there is a librarian or an individual interested in starting a library and this person goes about it correctly, some employees in the organization may think that the library has miraculously appeared.

To prepare users for the inauguration of library services, a public relations campaign is necessary. Prior to opening day, potential users should be supplied with library guides that provide sufficient information on services and collection development plans. Procedures for the use of the library including loan of materials, photocopy, and reference service should be spelled out. If forms for user registration are to be used, they should be available prior to the actual opening if possible. The librarian should work at building a degree of expectation on the part of future library users as the time approaches for service to begin. If the librarian is successful, everyone in the organization will know that library service is now available and that the library is a valuable addition to the organization.

Before this can happen, the librarian has to finish gathering the planning data to be used in decision making. Next, one can begin to work on setting goals for the library. Then the design of physical facilities and information services can proceed.

Appendix

The User Study: Sample Formats

Company XXX information needs survey questionnaire

As indicated in the accompanying letter from our president, information is playing an increasingly important role in the company's ability to develop and market effective and profitable products.

As part of the planning for a library to serve the employees of the company and to provide an effective and efficient response to information needs, a survey is being conducted.

Please respond to the following questions. Your answers will be considered confidential and individuals will not be identified in any of the data summaries. It is important that we know your information needs so that services can be offered that respond appropriately. The completed questionnaire is to be returned in the accompanying envelope to Room XXX no later than _____.

Thank you for your cooperation.

Name_____ Title_____

Department_____ Telephone_____

Questions about work environment

Questions listed here should identify the types of work for each individual, the amount of effort devoted to each, and information needs associated with each type.

Questions about current information use

This section should develop a list of questions to determine what information resources are currently needed and how these are obtained. If there are information needs that are going unmet, the consequences should be determined through appropriate questions. For example, are contracts lost? Did a product become obsolete? What was the monetary impact of not having the needed information?

Questions about information resources and services
that the individual would like to see as part of any information
or library service to be offered

Here you might choose to include the "shopping list" of available sources and services to aid the individual responding to the questions.

Thank you for taking the time to respond to these questions. Would you be willing to serve on a committee to aid in planning a library facility? We expect that such a committee will be formed within the next month and those interested will be invited to participate in the planning process.

Please return your completed questionnaire to Room XXX no later than _____.

User study: A sample shopping list
of information sources and services*

Dear Employee of Company XXX:

Please consider the following lists of information sources and services that could be made available in the library. Indicate the extent to which each of these might be useful to you in meeting your information needs:

---

*These lists are not meant to be all-inclusive; rather they indicate an approach that might be used in any one organization. The scale here is arbitrary and may not provide the information needed in a specific setting. For example, one might prefer to know the number of times that a source is used within a given time period. The construction of the forms and scales to be used should receive careful consideration. A pretest of all parts of the user study is necessary in order to eliminate misunderstandings or concerns about means of reporting responses.

List 1

	Need			
Source	*Daily*	*Weekly*	*Seldom*	*Never*
Chemical abstracts 1980 to date? Before 1980?	___	___	___	___
Biographic directories	___	___	___	___
Foreign language dictionaries	___	___	___	___
U.S. patent literature	___	___	___	___
Foreign patent literature	___	___	___	___
Government technical reports	___	___	___	___
Material classified for national security purposes	___	___	___	___
Science Citation Index	___	___	___	___
National standards and specifications	___	___	___	___
Foreign language journals (please specify titles for those consulted on a regular basis)	___	___	___	___
Please list additional sources important to your information needs (use an additional sheet if necessary)	___	___	___	___

List 2

Following are services that the library might provide. Please indicate
your need for each of these services.

Service	Daily	Weekly	Seldom	Never	Ranking*
		Need			
Ready reference service (providing names, addresses, spellings, quick facts, etc.)	___	___	___	___	___
Bibliographic searches involving complex subject searches	___	___	___	___	___
Single subject and author literature searches	___	___	___	___	___
Translation of foreign language material	___	___	___	___	___
An alerting service notifying you of information in your field on a regular and recurring basis without your asking for it	___	___	___	___	___
Orientation and instruction in the use of the library and information resources	___	___	___	___	___
Editing assistance by verification and formatting of bibliographic citations; Could also involve proofreading	___	___	___	___	___

*Rank on basis of importance, with 1 being a service that is most important.

Please list and describe any other services you might like to see provided by the library. Please give each service a number reflecting its importance to you. More than one service may be given a 1.

Cited Literature

Advanced Technology/Libraries. White Plains, N.Y.: Knowledge Industry 1972–. Monthly.

Ahrensfeld, J. L. et al., eds. *Special Libraries: A Guide for Management*. 2d rev. ed. Washington, D.C.: Special Libraries Association, 1986.

American Theological Library Association. *American Theological Library Association Newsletter*. Chicago: American Theological Library Association, 1953–. Quarterly.

Auri, Rao, and J. S. Robinson. *A Guide to U.S. Government Scientific & Technical Resources*. Littleton, Colo.: Libraries Unlimited, 1983.

Bare, C. E. "Conducting User Requirement Studies in Special Libraries." *Special Libraries* 57 (February 1966): 103–106.

Bradley, Janet, ed. *Hospital Library Management*. Chicago: Medical Library Association, 1983.

BRS Bulletin. Latham, N.Y.: BRS Information Technologies, 1979–. Monthly.

Bulletin of the Medical Library Association. Chicago: Medical Library Association, 1911–. Quarterly.

The Chronolog. Palo Alto: Dialog Information Services, Inc., 1973–. Monthly.

Darling, Louise, ed. *Handbook of Medical Library Practice*. 4th ed. Chicago: Medical Library Association, 1982–1988. 3 vols.

Darnay, B. T., ed. *Directory of Special Libraries and Information Centers*, 9th ed. Detroit: Gale Research Co., 1985.

Database. Weston, Conn.: Online, Inc., 1978–. Bimonthly.

Jackson, E. B., ed. *Special Librarianship*. Metuchen, N.J.: Scarecrow Press, 1980.

Lancaster, F. W. *The Measurement and Evaluation of Library Services*. Washington, D.C.: Information Resources Press, 1977.

Law Library Journal. Chicago: American Association of Law Libraries, 1908–. Quarterly.

Library Hi Tech. Ann Arbor: Pierian, 1984–. Monthly.

Music Library Association Newsletter. Canton, Mass.: 1969–. Quarterly.

Online. Weston, Conn.: Online, Inc., 1976–. Bimonthly.

The Reference Librarian. New York: Haworth, 1981–. Semiannual.

Roper, R.W., and J. A. Boorkman. *Introduction to Reference Sources in the Health Sciences*. 2d ed. Chicago: Medical Library Association, 1984.

RQ. Chicago: American Library Association, 1960–. Quarterly.

Science & Technology Libraries. New York: Haworth, 1980–. Quarterly.

Special Libraries. Washington, D.C.: Special Libraries Association, 1910–. Quarterly.

Subramanyam, Krishna. *Scientific and Technical Information Resources*. New York: Marcel Dekker, 1981.

Suggested Readings

Anderson, E. L., ed. *Newspaper Libraries in the U.S. and Canada.* 2d ed. New York: Special Libraries Association, 1980.

Bailey, M. J. "Functions of Selected Company Libraries/Information Centers." *Special Libraries* 72 (January 1981): 18–30.

Barnett, J. B. "Marine Science Libraries: A State of the Art Report." *Special Libraries* 75 (July 1984): 183–92.

Dillon, M. "Serving the Information Needs of Scientific Research." *Special Libraries* 72 (March 1981): 215–23.

Hull, D. "The Museum Library in the United States: A Sample." *Special Libraries* 67 (July 1976): 289–98.

Kenyon, K. A. "Zoo/Aquarium Libraries: A Survey." *Special Libraries* 75 (October 1984): 329–34.

Levin, E. J. "Establishing a Special Library: The First Year." *Special Libraries* 73 (July 1982): 193–201.

Mick, C. K. et al. "Toward Usable User Studies." *Journal of the American Society for Information Science* 31 (September 1980): 347–56.

Mount, E. *Special Libraries and Information Centers: An Introductory Text.* New York: Special Libraries Association, 1983.

Rees, A. M., and Susan Crawford. *Directory of Health Sciences Libraries in the U.S.* Cleveland: Case Western Reserve University, 1979.

St. Clair, G. "The One-Person Library: An Essay On Essentials Revisited." *Special Libraries* 78 (Fall 1987): 263–70.

Severson-Tris, M. A. "The Map Library in Private Industry: An Operating Example." *Special Libraries* 69 (March 1978): 94–99.

Steuermann, C. "Music Libraries." *Special Libraries* 69 (November 1978): 425–28.

Stueart, R. D., and B. B. Moran. *Library Management* 3d ed. Littleton, Colo.: Libraries Unlimited, 1987.

Voigt, M. J. *Scientists' Approaches to Information.* Chicago: American Library Association, 1961.

Walker, W. B. "Art Libraries: International and Interdisciplinary." *Special Libraries* 69 (December 1978): 476–81.

Wright, W. F. "Information Management: A Bibliography." *Special Libraries* 73 (October 1982): 298–310.

2 Functioning as a Manager

There are a number of managerial functions that must be performed in any library, even the very small library. The success with which these functions are executed may be even more critical in determining the future of the very small library than would be the case with a larger, well-staffed library. In a small library constant demands are made upon every minute of staff time and it is easy to put aside the managerial aspects of library operation and concentrate instead on the regular daily routines of circulation and reference. However, to ignore these highly important management functions will only lead to stagnant and uneven service to library users. The goals of library service cannot be met if the librarian fails to provide planned direction for the library. A number of different managerial functions will be discussed throughout this chapter, but many writers agree that there are at least four functions common to all organizations. These include organizing, planning, directing, and controlling.

Organizing

Organizing is a basic managerial function, and in libraries it is generally associated with the book and periodical collections. In a larger sense, organizing has to do with defining and explaining the relationships between different operational units and between different persons within an organization. The librarian must be particularly concerned with the relationship between the library as an organization-wide information resource and its placement within the formal structure of the parent organization or institution. The library should be placed in the organizational hierarchy along with similar service units, or with the units of its principal users. One often finds the library in the branch responsible for research and development. In this situation, the librarian reports directly to the individuals most dependent upon the services that the library provides.

As a general rule, it is best for the librarian to report to a person in as high a position as possible within the organization. However, if the person to whom the librarian reports is too busy to give adequate thought and encouragement to the library's development, then reporting to someone in a lower position who is interested in promoting the library's welfare may be a preferable alternative. In either case, the librarian will need to have ready access to individuals with appropriate decision-making authority.

The organization chart is a graphic means by which the place of the library within the parent organization can be seen. The chart should clearly show the reporting lines and the means by which the library aids in the overall attainment of the organization's goals. The librarian of the small library needs to make sure that the library is included on such a chart. It is usually not necessary for the very small library to have an organization chart of its own. Once a library begins to grow and its functions are divided between different individuals, then an organization chart becomes useful. Sample organization charts showing various means of placing the library within the parent organization are included in many library science monographs, including the one by Stueart and Moran.

Planning

Planning is the second managerial function and it is undoubtedly one of the most important ways in which the very small library can ensure its growth and future. Planning is necessary if the library is to continue to achieve its goals and to support the goals of the larger organization or institution.

Planning is an ongoing process as are organizing, directing, and controlling. These functions are also interactive, so that decisions concerning any one aspect of library operation also influence the direction and decision making with regard to other managerial functions. For example, if the planning process leads to a new service for users, that decision limits the amount of time and resources available for other new or existing services as long as other factors remain constant.

Planning must precede the creation of a library and for this reason it is very important that the position of librarian be filled as far in advance of the opening of the library as possible. A minimum of six months lead time is recommended to prepare library facilities that are based on a sound study of potential user needs, to design appropriate user services, to acquire and organize the opening day collection, and to have everything in place on opening day. However, it is not always possible for the librarian to have this time, and planning may have to go hand in hand with the establishment and operation of a library. In such case, the librarian may just have to make do initially until planning can lead to improvement.

Planning does not end with the opening of the library. The ongoing planning function involves two aspects. One of these is the development of a plan for the attainment of the library's goals over an extended period, possibly three to five years. This is known as long-range or strategic planning. Long-range planning provides a general strategy for the library's development. Such planning may also be directed at some specific future event such as the addition of space to the library or the initiation of a new user service. It should be stressed that the long-range plan is not a permanent document, although the plan should be put in writing. The plan needs to be constantly reevaluated in light of changes in the library's environment and with respect to broader organization goals. As each year in the long-range plan is completed and evaluated, the remainder of the plan should be adjusted as necessary and then projected yet another year into the future.

Plan approval

The long-range plan for the library must receive the approval of top management within the organization. This plan will be the basis for future budget predictions and requests, and the librarian will use the long-range plan as a blueprint for the future. For the plan, the librarian must be able to predict what the library's future needs will be and also be able to state why future library development will be necessary.

Operational planning

The second planning aspect concentrates on the operation of the library during the current fiscal year. This is called operational planning, and it involves formulation of the budget for the coming year, identification of the day-to-day problems of library operation, and investigation of solutions that will lead to the attainment of the short-range objectives of the library. This type of planning concerns work load projections and the management of funds already committed for library operations.

The day-to-day planning process involves identifying the best solutions to the problems encountered in providing information services. This necessitates the clear identification of a problem, for example, how to improve the acquisitions process, how to shorten the time required for receipt of interlibrary loans, or how to provide a service that brings new information to the attention of those who might have need for it. Once the problem has been clearly specified and separated from related problems, then the creative process begins. This involves the delineation of possible solutions and a detailed analysis of each alternative in terms of its cost, benefits, and disadvantages, to the library as well as its advantages and disadvantages to library users. Once appropriate alternatives have been identified and examined, one of these alternatives or a combination can be selected as a plan of action.

One of the problems faced by the librarian in the very small library is the lack of direct communication with other librarians who might be of assistance in identifying possible alternative solutions. Thus, visits to other libraries may be of some value in this creative part of the planning process. Librarians as a group are enthusiastic in their willingness to share. Library literature may or may not be useful, depending on the problem under consideration.

The final part of the planning process is deciding how the outcome is to be evaluated once a plan of action has been implemented. This is important in determining whether or not a problem has been solved. A discussion of evaluation techniques can be found in chapter 12.

Directing

Directing is the one managerial function that will probably not have much importance for the manager of a very small library. This function involves the personal interaction between supervisors and staff members. Even though the directing function may not take too much time, the librarian should still be aware of the basic motivational concepts that influence the work environment and also of the various techniques in employee evaluation. Knowledge of motivational concepts will provide the librarian with some insights into the motivation of library users, and knowledge of employee evaluation techniques will be useful in determining how well the librarian is performing in the provision of library services. The use of volunteers in the very small library will be discussed in chapter 4. Directing may play a part in the supervision of this type of library worker.

Controlling

Controlling is the fourth managerial function. This function concerns monitoring library performance. It is through the controlling process that appropriate measurements, statistical and otherwise, are taken and then evaluated to determine the library's attainment of its objectives. This is an extremely important and sometimes difficult function for the manager of the small library who must not only make the measurements but must also gather the required data on a day-to-day basis. This is often a menial and time-consuming process, and it will require the utmost attention in the very small library in order to ensure that accurate and complete data are recorded. An earlier discussion dealt with evaluation as part of the planning function in which different alternatives are evaluated. In such cases there are no operating data with which to make an evaluation. The librarian uses data and opinions from the library or outside sources. Evaluation as part of the controlling function involves the use of actual operating data derived from plans that have been put into effect. Hard data, such as the number of reference questions answered on a day-to-day basis, are used as measurements for such evaluation.

Once data have been gathered, they must be compared to some pre-established standard of performance in order to see whether the library's objectives have been achieved. Before this measurement can take place, the library must first have a clear, written statement of goals and objectives.

Goals

Goals may be seen as occupying the upper level of an imaginary operational hierarchy. Goals are broad, abstract ideas about what the library wants to achieve. Library goals should reflect the goals of the parent organization. For example, the goals of an organization concerned with making profits will be to expand markets, develop new products, utilize an inexpensive and dependable work force, implement efficient management practices, and develop capital resources to meet the expanding needs of the organization. The library's goals will need to reflect these organizational goals.

The goals for any library should clearly define the nature of the library and the population being served—public, academic, school, or special library. Regardless of the type of library and the need to reflect organizational goals, certain aspects are more or less common to all types of libraries. These include the need for goals relating to the physical facilities, collection development and organization, user services, financial support, staff retention and development, library management, and library cooperation. Other specialized goals may also be appropriate depending upon the mission of a particular library. Most important is that the library's goals relate as directly as possible to the achievement of the overall organizational goals.

Objectives

Just below "goals" in the imaginary hierarchy would be the listed objectives. Objectives are operational statements about what the library is to do within a specific period of time. The achievement of objectives is the means by which goals are to be attained. Objectives should be written as statements of measurable outcomes. The extent to which an objective can be expressed in quantifiable terms will determine the ease with which it can be measured. Even so, qualitative measurements also have a part to play in many library objectives; it is just more difficult to measure the accuracy or quality of something than to count the number of occurrences. Objectives should be written in such a way that the predicted level of performance is included as part of the objective statement. This predicted level of performance or standard of performance varies, of course, from objective to objective and usually from measurement period to measurement period.

Goals are usually very abstract; objectives are very specific. For example, an objective in which standards of performance are clearly stated is that "the library will provide at least 250 searches in the coming year." In this example, there is no upper limit to the number of searches that might be performed, but the expectation is that no fewer than 250 searches will be conducted. Measurement of the attainment of this objective will involve comparison of the actual number of searches performed against the original objective statement.

Of necessity, one has to assume that the attainment of specific objectives will lead to the achievement of the goals to which they relate. The goal statement for the above objective might include something to the effect that the library will meet user information needs in an efficient and timely fashion.

Once acceptable goals and objectives covering all aspects of the library's operation have been written, the means of achieving them must be considered. It should be emphasized first, however, that for any one goal there may be dozens of objectives formulated as the means for achieving that one goal. Objectives, in turn, are achieved through policies, procedures, and individual tasks. The picture of this imaginary hierarchy would appear as follows:

GOALS
   OBJECTIVES
      POLICIES
         PROCEDURES
            TASKS

The importance of the managerial function of planning should be apparent at each of the different levels in this hierarchy.

Policies

Policies are intended to guide decision making and provide a consistent basis for the library's operation. Policies tend to reflect the intent or rationale of the objectives to which they apply, thus it may be possible to describe a given policy as being either restrictive or permissive, or a combination of both. For example, if the objective is to provide library materials to users where and when they are needed, this will require circulation policies that allow materials to be checked out to the locations where they will be used (permissive). It will also require an effective recall policy to ensure that materials will be available when they are needed for other users (restrictive). In this case, the policies are both permissive and restrictive in order to achieve the circulation objective.

Procedures

Procedures are actual work routines to be performed in accordance with established policies. For example, the circulation procedure for checking out materials to an individual is guided by circulation policies. In most libraries, individual job descriptions are made up of several different procedures. In the very small library, all procedures may be performed by one individual. Still, it is just as important that the same amount of planning and detail go into these policies and procedures as in a larger, well-staffed library. Policies that are intelligent and clearly spelled out save time, as do carefully planned work procedures.

Tasks

Individual tasks are the separate steps that together make up a procedure. In the circulation example above, verification of the status of a borrower would be one step in the procedure to check out materials.

Careful attention to the functions of organizing, planning, directing, and controlling will ensure an effective and efficient operation ranging from the performance of individual tasks to the attainment of overall library goals. Time taken from actual library operations to devote to these managerial functions will ultimately result in the considerable saving of time. Remember that time is of the utmost importance in the very small library.

Before considering how library operations are to be financed, please refer to the following examples of goals and objectives and how these can be ordered into an operational hierarchy.

Appendix

Goals and Objectives

Here is a list of general goals that might apply to almost any very small library. These can be modified to define the characteristics of a particular discipline. In addition, specialized goals pertaining to a specific library might also be added to this list.

Goals

To provide a physical facility that houses the collection and allows for several years growth while providing ample and effective user space.

To acquire and organize a collection of current information resources regardless of format so that users' needs can be met in an efficient manner.

To provide information services that meet the needs of all individuals in the organization and contribute effectively to the development and marketing of new products.

To recruit, train, develop, and retain a staff with skills necessary to provide the best information services and support functions possible.

To provide a detailed and justified plan for the financial management of the library and its planned growth.

To operate with a system of management that ensures accountability for the library and meets the human needs of those employed therein.

To actively participate in cooperative arrangements with other libraries and utilities in order to expand access to information resources regardless of where they are located.

Objectives

Each of the above goals might well have a dozen or more objectives devoted to it. The librarian should write as many as needed in order to measure the attainment of a particular goal.

The following is an example of the operational hierarchy proceeding from a single goal to the ultimate tasks that contribute to its achievement.

Goal: To provide information where and when it is needed to all users of the library on an equal basis.

Objectives: To provide a circulation, hold, and recall system that makes monographs available for use in offices and laboratories.

To provide photocopy facilities that enable users to make copies of journal articles for their own use.

To acquire materials not owned by the library through cooperative arrangements with other libraries and vendors.

Policies for these objectives: Monographs shall circulate for a period of two weeks and may be renewed once.

Monographs that have passed the initial two week circulation period may be recalled if another user places a hold on that material.

Journals will not circulate.

Coin-operated photocopy machines will be placed in user areas.

Anyone may request an interlibrary loan for materials not owned by the library. The librarian will determine the best means of securing the needed material.

(Many additional policies may be needed to make the stated objectives operational).

Procedures (only one procedure will be listed): Recalling a monograph needed by another user.

Tasks: (User requests item not on shelf.)

Check in circulation file to determine date due.

Have user fill out hold request.

Notify user that another person has placed a hold on item checked out to him/her.

When item is returned, clear record and notify user that item is available.

Place on hold shelf.

Check out material to user who placed hold.

Cited Literature

Stueart, R. D., and B. B. Moran. *Library Management.* 3d ed. Littleton, Colo.: Libraries Unlimited, 1987.

Suggested Readings

Barnum, S. J. "Characteristics and Management of a Small Special Library." *Il-*

linois Libraries 62 (March 1980): 223–25.

Bauer, C. K. "Managing Management." *Special Libraries* 71 (April 1980): 204–16.

Berner, A. "The Importance of Time Management in the Small Library." *Special Libraries* 78 (Fall 1987): 271–76.

Cao, J. F. "Managing the Technical Library." In *Current Concepts in Library Management.* Littleton, Colo.: Libraries Unlimited, 1979. 131–56.

Holladay, J. "Small Libraries: Keeping the Professional Position Professional." *Special Libraries* 72 (January 1981): 63–66.

Katayama, J. H. "The Library Committee." *Special Libraries* 44 (January 1983): 44–48.

Morris, J. *The Library Disaster Preparedness Handbook.* Chicago: American Library Association, 1986.

St. Clair, Guy, and Joan Williamson. *Managing the One-Person Library.* Stoneham, Mass.: Butterworth, 1986.

Schiller, F., and G. H. Merritt. "The Hospital Library Committee." *Bulletin of the Medical Library Association* 55 (July 1967): 321–23.

Sinclair, D. M. *Administration of the Small Public Library.* 2d ed. Chicago: American Library Association, 1979.

Special Libraries Association. "Objectives and Standards for Special Libraries." *Special Libraries* 21 (December 1964): 671–80.

Stanton, R. O. "Applying the Management-By-Objectives Technique in an Industrial Library." *Journal of the American Society for Information Science* 26 (November 1975): 313–17.

White, H. S. *Managing the Special Library: Strategies for Success within the Larger Organization.* White Plains, N.Y.: Knowledge Industry Publications, 1984.

3 Financing
Library Operations

The financial administration of the very small library provides the life blood for the library *money*. It establishes the controls that are required to ensure the effective use of monies received, and monitors the librarian's accountability for monies received and expended. Financial management requires rather extensive record keeping and this may bother the manager of the very small library because so much time must be spent seeking funds for the library and then keeping an accurate record of how these funds are used. There really are no shortcuts since the utilization of financial resources allocated to the library relates directly to the attainment of the library's goals. The librarian should always put forth an extreme effort when it comes to financial resources for the library.

The focus of this chapter is on different types of budgets that might be of use in the very small library, the record keeping systems that are necessary to control expenditures, and the need to report on the financial status of the library's accounts. It should be pointed out that librarians of many small libraries do not become actively involved in the budgeting process; this is frequently done for them by the parent organization. In some instances the librarian is free to expend whatever monies are needed for collection development, supplies, and equipment. In other cases, large expenditures, often called capital expenditures, require some prior approval before orders can be placed. This approach to funding is fine if the flow of money is unending and its continuance assured. Unfortunately, such is not usually the case, and the librarian may be left in a position of never knowing just what monies will be available for what types of expenditures. Such an informal system may work well in good times, but when the parent organization becomes pressed for funds, the librarian may be left in a position of uncertainty. If the librarian is to plan the library's goals and the means of achieving them, then a carefully prepared financial plan is required.

Types of budgets

Several different types of budgets have evolved over the years in a variety of organizations and all of these are applicable in one type of library or another. A very small library could employ any one of these budgets. It is common to find that a variety of features from a number of different types of budgets have been combined. Among the commonly recognized budgets with some applicability for the small library are the lump sum, line-item, object of expenditure, formula, program, and performance. Two types more recently in vogue have been the planning, programming, budgeting system (PPBS) and the zero-based budget. The suitability of all of these types of budgets for the very small library will be discussed briefly.

The lump sum budget will be eliminated from this discussion because it is only relevant when some higher authority sets aside a certain sum to be used for library operations. Any budgeting approach that does not consider the possible sources of library income and the variety of expense items in arriving at a budget figure is not really a useful budgeting practice, rather, it is arbitrary and may result in a capricious allocation of funds. Managers of very small libraries who find themselves operating with a lump sum budget should work to become actively involved in the formulation of the library's budget so that an alternative budgeting system can be used.

The line-item budget

The line-item budget is one of the simplest to prepare and has been widely used in all types of libraries. In this approach, each item of expenditure is specified on a line along with the amount requested for that item of expenditure. Table 3.1 illustrates the materials category of a budget in which a specific amount is

Table 3.1

Line Items for a Library Materials Budget

Library Materials	*Amount Budgeted*
Monographs	$1,500
Serials	5,000
Technical reports	850
Patents	350
Newsletters	150
	$7,850

indicated for each of the five types of materials (or lines) in this category.

The line-item budget lends itself to close accountability for funds expended. Either the amount budgeted was spent for the item in question or it was not. Consequently, the librarian has little flexibility in making adjustments within the budget. For example, the librarian may find that there are not enough worthwhile monographs published during the year to warrant spending the full $1,500 in the above illustration. The librarian might prefer to take some of the monograph monies and put them toward additional periodical subscriptions as part of the serials line, but this is not possible with a line-item budget. Funds cannot be shifted between lines unless permission is obtained from the authority responsible for authorizing the budget.

The object of expenditure budget

In the object of expenditure budget, the line items are collapsed into categories, or objects of expenditure, as shown in the following example.

Object of Expenditure Budget

Objects	*Amount Budgeted*
Acquisitions	$7,850

In this budget, all five types of materials from the line-item budget (monographs, serials, technical reports, patents, newsletters) have been included in the amount requested for "Acquisitions." The librarian is free to make allocations to be expended for each of these types of materials. The only restriction is that no more than $7,850 may be spent to acquire materials for the library's collection. Because of the flexibility of the object of expenditure budget as compared to the line-item budget, the librarian is better able to determine how funds are to be spent. The object of expenditure budget is an easy budget to prepare. This can be misleading, however, because the ease of budget preparation may not reflect the usefulness of the budget being prepared. Library objectives and programs should and do change from year to year and this must be reflected in the library's budget. Object of expenditure budgets usually employ last year's budget as a starting point for the next year's budget. Adding on an additional percentage figure each year may simplify the budgeting process, but it may not reflect the changing budget needs required to meet changing library goals.

The formula budget

The formula budget is based on key variables that relate to library operation or aspects of the larger institution. These variables may be enrollment, the number of personnel employed, the number of units produced, or similar quantifiable aspects. Such budgets are usually easy to formulate once the variables have been identified and quantified. A popular method often used as a base in formula budgeting has been to allot the library a specified dollar amount for each student enrolled or for each company employee. This approach ensures budget growth as the number of potential library users increases. A small public library might receive a budget based on a formula derived from a per capita calculation. Here, the relationship between the variables used in the formula and the attainment of the library's goals and objectives is of concern. How the money allocated through the formula relates to this attainment is not always clear. In summary, formula budgeting may work well in good times, but it may greatly restrict the library's performance under adverse economic conditions. Formulas also invite manipulation as a means of securing more and more funds. For example, an individual may seek to adjust the formula using different bases in the calculation until the most advantageous formula is found without any regard for the relationship between funding and goal achievement.

The program budget

The program budget (see Table 3.2) is a popular type of budgeting practice found in a variety of different types of libraries of all sizes. Its popularity is largely based on its degree of accountability, its flexibility in terms of budget management, and its attempt to allocate income and expenses to specific library objectives. The program budget considers the amount of income generated by each library program as well as the expenses that must be apportioned to each program. Some of the programs a small library might wish to budget for include reference services, circulation of materials, acquisition and processing of materials, organizing the collection, photocopying services, and online information services. Varying amounts for salaries, equipment, supplies, environmental costs (rent and utilities), and other related expenses are computed for each program and the sum of all programs would be the total amount requested in the program budget.

The performance budget

The performance budget is very similar in preparation to the program budget with the main difference being the format in which the final budget is presented. The performance budget process concentrates on the amount required to achieve a particular library objective at a given level of performance. For example, an

Table 3.2

Abbreviated Program Budget Format (two programs)

Library Program	Income*	Expenses	Budget Request
Online information services	$8,000		
Personnel		$ 6,000	
Training		850	
Equipment		875	
Supplies		25	
Telecommunications		1,000	
Database charges		2,500	
Totals	8,000	10,650	$2,650
Circulation of materials	750		
Personnel		3,000	
Equipment		500	
Supplies		300	
Computer charges		800	
Totals	750	4,600	3,850

*Because income will be generated throughout the budget period, the organization or institution will have to advance this amount in operating funds and then when income is actually derived, it can be used to repay these advances. The income under the Online Information Services Program might be generated by user charges for searches performed. The income under the Circulation of Materials Program might be the result of fines assessed for overdue materials.

objective of almost every small library is to provide short answers to factual questions. This is the so-called "ready reference" objective. Imagine that a particular library anticipates that it will be necessary to answer some 600 ready reference questions during the coming year. In order to arrive at this figure, estimates will be based on past performance statistics and the librarian's best guess as to what the future holds in store. In an attempt to arrive at a budget figure for the cost of providing these 600 answers, performance budgeting first determines the cost of answering one ready reference question. This figure, the basic unit cost, is multiplied by 600 to arrive at a budget figure for the coming year. For example, if it can be determined that it costs $3.00 to answer one ready reference question during the current year, then it is possible to estimate that in order to answer 600 such questions next year, the budget will need to include a figure of $1,800 to meet this objective. Of course, the librarian will also want to include an additional amount to cover any inflation factors that may occur from one budget period to another. In a similar fashion, basic unit costs can be determined for all aspects of library operation. Some of the procedures for which costs might be computed include the acquisition of different types of library material, the cataloging of each item acquired, processing of single items added to the collection, the circulation of an item, the answering of reference questions, conducting an online search, and the acquisition of an interlibrary loan.

The record keeping required by performance budgeting can be very involved and time consuming, but it is especially worthwhile for the librarian in the very small library. This type of careful analysis provides insights into library operations that are not readily available through other less demanding budgeting practices. This budget approach lends credibility to the library's need for the amounts being requested. In addition, it increases the librarian's accountability because the objectives budgeted include levels of performance and it is easy for the authorizing body to check back and see whether these performance levels were achieved. In the unfortunate event that the amounts requested are not funded in full, this type of budget makes it easier to reduce performance levels by cutting back on the number of basic units to be produced. The very small library can be called on more frequently than almost any other size library or organizational unit to justify its existence. This is particularly true for libraries in the private sector. It is only through the careful gathering and analysis of cost and performance information that justification can be documented. Therefore, it is appropriate for even the most hard-pressed librarian to pay particular attention to the financial aspects of library management. Other types of budgets may be easier to construct and administer, but their lack of attention to the relationship between expenses and the attainment of objectives often make them less desirable than the performance budget.

The planning, programming, budgeting system (PPBS)

The planning, programming, budgeting system (PPBS) appears to have evolved from performance budgeting practices with which it has more similarities than differences. One difference, however, is the emphasis of PPBS on long-range objectives in the budgeting process. This emphasis is certainly worthwhile and underscores the relationship between budgeting and planning, but one must be cautious in making long-range economic projections in an unstable economy. In any event, the emphasis of PPBS on the cost/effectiveness/benefit of any given library objective draws attention to the benefits being received for the funds expended. With PPBS, attention is given to the qualitative side of evaluating objectives. This approach is largely missing in the other budgeting practices discussed up to now. For example, in planning for the implementation of a new online bibliographic search service, one would set out with a clear understanding of the objective of such a program. It is likely that full implementation of the service can take two or more years. A PPBS approach would mean that full cost data for both direct and indirect expenses be identified as part of the initial planning and budgeting. Various means of providing the service would be examined in a detailed cost/effectiveness/ benefit analysis of each alternative. Such an approach compares costs against how well each alternative works when contrasted to the value of achieving the objective. Based on such an analysis, the alternative selected can be budgeted with accuracy over the period required for implementation.

The zero-based budget

One of the newer approaches to budgeting is the zero-based budget process. Quite simply, the aim of this approach is to reexamine each objective for each budget period so that programs that should no longer be funded will not be continued. This method ensures that the library's objectives are evaluated periodically and the order of priority reestablished for each new budget. Some objectives may be phased out; others may receive increased or decreased funding; others may remain at the same funding level as in the previous budget period. Because the priority of objectives is established at various levels throughout the organizational hierarchy, starting at the bottom and working up, the final selection and funding level for individual organizational units is compatible with overall organizational goals. The result is an organizational budget that builds from the bottom, or zero base, upward.

Any of the budgeting processes discussed above will work for the very small library. It is likely that organizational policy regarding budget format will determine which of these approaches is used by the librarian. The important thing to remember in managing the very small library is the usefulness for management purposes of the data that are produced through the performance budget and program budget approaches, even if the librarian chooses or is required to present the budget in a different form.

Record-keeping systems

Once a library budget has been approved, it is imperative that accurate records of expenditures for that budget be kept. The librarian is responsible for monies expended, and sufficient documentation must be available to substantiate the legality of these expenditures. The librarian must assume that the record keeping systems of vendors and others with whom the library does business will not always be accurate and that some means of checking on these accounts must be maintained.

Because of the great amount of time involved in such record keeping, it is preferable if the librarian can rely on the organizational or institutional business office to maintain accurate, up-to-date records for the library. A basic requirement of record keeping in any library is that the librarian must always be able to know the exact amount left unspent and unencumbered in any of the library's accounts. Unfortunately, many business offices cannot or will not provide the needed currency of information, so similar records must also be maintained in the library. Since the librarian is responsible for managing the money in the library's budget, if the record keeping of others does not meet the librarian's needs, then record systems must be maintained within the library.

Requisitions, purchase orders, packing slips, and invoices

The day-to-day operation of the very small library will generate a number of different purchase-related documents, and records of these must be maintained. Requisitions are specific requests for goods and services that the library wishes to purchase. They specify exactly the items desired and in many organizations are sent on to central purchasing where the item is officially ordered. If the library is able to order directly, then time may be saved in the receipt of orders. However, centralized purchasing of some items usually results in financial savings. The actual order for an item is placed on a numbered purchase order and this is sent to the supplier. A copy of this purchase order should be sent to the library from central purchasing and retained for the library's records along with a copy of any requisition issued by the library. If the library can issue its own purchase orders, then the requisition step is omitted.

When ordered items are received, particularly in the case of books, packing slips will be included with the shipment. These need to be checked to determine the completeness of the shipment. Packing slips should be retained along with the purchase order until an invoice is received. The invoice is a bill for the goods received, and it should be checked against the purchase order and the packing slip to assure accuracy and completeness. One is only required to pay for items actually received.

All of this record keeping and checking makes demands on the scarce time of the librarian in the very small library. One possible alternative is to delegate some of this work to a centralized purchasing department. Although such a department may be willing to receive goods for the library and check them for correctness and completeness, library books and journals often present unique problems in identification and these usually require the expertise of the librarian for proper verification. In addition, judgments about the condition of shipments may vary depending upon whether the decision is that of a librarian or a shipping room clerk. Often, attempts to save the librarian's time through the use of outside helpers may actually cause more loss of time in the long run.

Records for basic unit costs

Records will also have to be maintained to document work load measures such as the number of books cataloged, the number of online searches conducted, and the number of items circulated. These records, along with those for expenditures, will be required when budget preparation begins. It may also be useful to keep some record of the actual expenditure of the librarian's time for various library functions. Estimates may be good enough for most applications, but there will be occasions when it is necessary to know exactly how much time was spent on a particular library function.

Inventory

Inventory records are needed to document the physical property of the library, including such things as typewriters, tables, and desks. It should not take much of the librarian's time to keep these records and to check periodically for the physical presence of items on the inventory. However, an inventory record of the library collection is neither maintained nor checked so easily. Most libraries maintain a shelf list, which is a card file that identifies all the titles and copies of materials cataloged in the collection. Checking this record against the physical presence of each item is time consuming and a nearly impossible task for someone in a very small library to perform alone. However, some sort of inventory must be done periodically, because as with the monetary resources of the library, the librarian is also responsible for all materials in the library's collection.

It is imperative that a librarian assuming a new library position complete an inventory of the existing collection as soon as possible. The new librarian may find that even though library records indicate a collection of twelve thousand volumes, an inventory reveals that several hundred of these cannot be accounted for. It is a matter of self-protection to document the true state of the collection at the time one assumes responsibility for it.

If complete inventory procedures are not feasible, then periodic random sampling of the collection may have to suffice. For example, a sample of 10 percent of the collection randomly selected and checked against the shelf list, the shelves, and other possible locations may give a reasonable estimate of the extent of loss in the collection. An even better approach is to use two independent random samples and compare the results. This method adds credibility to loss figures if the results are approximately the same for each sample. Even when sampling techniques are employed, it may still be useful to inventory parts of the collection more fully. For example, the reference collection should be inventoried periodically in its entirety, probably at least once a year.

Records of unmet user needs

A final type of record that can be highly useful in evaluating library performance and in planning for future directions is one of requests that the library is unable to meet. These records might include requests for materials that the library was unable to purchase, or questions it was unable to answer. Keeping and using such records enables the librarian to perform on ongoing user study and to plan accordingly.

Financial accounting and reporting

Monthly reports may or may not be required by organizational or institutional policy. Even if a monthly report is not called for, it may still be useful for the librarian to prepare one as an aid in summarizing the financial activity during that period. This type of monthly review is helpful to the librarian in the same way that monthly profit and loss statements serve the needs of the business world. The monthly report should indicate for each library account the original amount requested in the budget, the amount actually received, the amount expended to date, the amount encumbered, and the unspent, unencumbered balance. (Encumbered means simply that these funds have been set aside for orders that have been placed but not completed.) Once again, such record keeping and reporting takes away some of the valuable time of the person managing the very small library, but good management practices such as record keeping may also save time for the librarian. By referring to the monthly financial statement, the librarian can determine whether or not monies are available in any given account. This record may serve as an interim check until such time as the harried librarian can bring each account up-to-date through posting of individual transactions.

Annual reports

Annual financial reports may also be required of the librarian. The reports may be part of a larger comprehensive annual report or it may be a separate statement submitted along with the budget request for the coming year. Such a report is important as part of performance budgeting because it helps measure whether objectives were achieved in the preceding year. Please refer to the end of this chapter for examples of monthly and annual financial reports.

Insurance

A final note needs to be added to any discussion of finances, and that has to do with insurance for the library. A library requires insurance for two purposes beyond the provision of physical safeguards and benefits for library staff. One is to ensure that anyone who enters the library is protected in case of personal injury; the other is to ensure that any part of the collection that might be destroyed or damaged can be replaced (including the cost of acquisition and processing in addition to the actual purchase cost of the materials). Chances are good that the institutional or organizational insurance policies, which include the library, are sufficient at least with regard to the library's first requirement, but this should be verified. It will probably be necessary for the librarian to check to make sure that coverage is adequate for the library's collection as well. Books and journals cannot be replaced with the same ease as chairs and tables, and it is the librarian's responsibility to be sure that the library is adequately covered. One should never insure in excess of actual replacement costs, including processing costs, because this results in higher premiums. Insurance policies should be maintained on a renewal frequency that keeps up with the changing value of items insured.

Appendix

Financial Reports

Monthly financial statement: Line-item budget

Line item	Amount budgeted	Amount received	Expended	Encumbered	Unspent/ unencumbered
Personnel					
Librarian	$22,000	$22,000	$18,000	$ 4,000	$ 00
Library Materials					
Monographs	7,500	7,000	5,800	400	800
Serials	15,000	15,000	00	15,000	00
Audiovisuals	3,000	3,000	2,700	100	200
Supplies					
Library supplies	1,000	1,000	800	150	50
Office supplies	300	300	280	00	20
Equipment					
Library equipment	900	750	650	50	50
Office equipment	400	400	400	00	00

Annual financial statement:
Performance budget

Objective	Amount budgeted	Amount received	Amount expended	Basic units projected	Basic units produced	Basic unit cost
Circulation	$ 27,000	$27,000	$27,000	80,000	87,000	$ 0.31
Acquisitions	104,000	99,000	99,000	2,750	2,750	36.00
Interlibrary loan						
Borrowing	10,000	10,000	9,000	182	164	5.50
Lending	7,000	7,000	8,000	145	166	4.80
Reference Service						
Ready ref	17,000	17,000	17,000	4,600	4,800	3.54
Manual search	3,000	3,000	900	300	78	11.54
Online search	15,000	15,000	17,000	1,175	2,013	8.49

Suggested Readings

Bonnell, P. *Fund Raising for the Small Library*. Chicago: American Library Association, 1983.

Clark, P. M. *Microcomputer Spreadsheet Models for Libraries: Preparing Documents, Budgets, and Statistical Reports*. Chicago: American Library Association, 1985.

Corfield, W. "Key to Public Library Budgeting." *Canadian Library Journal* 35 (October 1978): 349–51.

Corry, E. *Grants for Libraries: A Guide to Public and Private Funding Programs and Proposal Writing Techniques*. Littleton, Colo.: Libraries Unlimited, 1982.

Geddes, A. *Fiscal Responsibility and the Small Public Library*. Chicago: American Library Association, 1978.

George, M. R. "Budget Planning." *Catholic Library World* 48 (April 1977): 368–81.

Koenig, M. E. D. "Budgets and Budgeting." *Special Libraries* 68 (July/August 1977): 228–40.

————. *Budgeting Techniques for Libraries and Information Centers*. New York: Special Libraries Association, 1980.

Kountz, J. "Library Cost Analysis: A Recipe." *Library Journal* 97 (February 1, 1972): 459–64.

Maybury, C. "Performance Budgeting for the Library." *ALA Bulletin* 55 (January 1961): 46–53.

Prentice, A. E. *Public Library Finance*. Chicago: American Library Association, 1977.

Sargent, C. W. "Zero-base Budgeting and the Library." *Bulletin of the Medical Library Association* 66 (January 1978): 31–35.

Sellers, D. Y. "Basic Planning and Budgeting Concepts for Special Libraries." *Special Libraries* 64 (February 1973): 70–75.

Smith, G. S. *Accounting for Librarians and Other Non-profit Managers*. Chicago: American Library Association, 1983.

Trumpeter, M. C., and R. S. Rounds. *Basic Budgeting Practices for Librarians*. Chicago: American Library Association, 1985.

Wagenveld, L. M. "Doing More With Less." *Special Libraries* 78 (Winter 1987): 16–20.

White, H. S. "The Funding of Corporate Libraries—Old Myths and New Problems." *Special Libraries* 78 (Summer 1987): 155–61.

4 Staffing the Library

It should be evident that the most important resource in the very small library is time—the time of the librarian. This chapter will look at ways in which the staffing of the very small library can be improved even though money is not available for adding more staff.

The workweek

Many people assume that a forty-hour workweek for the librarian will mean an eight to five schedule. But this arrangement may not be the best way to achieve the library's objectives. Librarians should strive to be available when they are needed, not just to match some arbitrary schedule. In a newspaper library, for example, the rush for information may be in the few hours before the next edition's deadline. If the paper is to be distributed in a morning edition, then the greatest need for information by reporters may be in the evening hours. It might be that the hospital librarian needs to be present on weekends because that is the time when most admissions are made and the need for information is the greatest. A librarian should consider the following questions when planning a schedule. When do library users frequent the library? At what times during the day or evening do users need a librarian to assist them? And by contrast, what is the best time for the librarian to proceed without interruption in the variety of library operations that do not directly involve interaction with library users?

Depending upon company or institutional policies, and the librarian's needs and inclinations, it may be possible to set aside a few hours when the library is closed to allow the librarian to make maximum use of her time performing tasks such as acquisitions, cataloging, budgeting, planning, and reporting. The remainder of the librarian's workday can be scheduled for those times when patrons are most likely to come to the library or call the library for help. If the library cannot be closed to allow the librarian to perform other duties, it should still be possible to identify slow times and target them for periods of concentrated work. Uninterrupted periods of sustained effort are more likely to be productive than short periods when one has to attend to the task at hand while answering the telephone, checking out books, etc.

Library hours

In some organizations the library must be available at all times to meet users' information needs. Such is often the case in a hospital library, but the same may apply to a law firm, an engineering concern, or any other type of organization where staff and employees are not limited to a traditional daytime schedule. While small public libraries do not need to be always accessible, they probably need to offer extensive after-work hours to accommodate many of their users. One approach to continuous access is to leave the library open or available at all times. Under very special conditions the library might even be designed without doors at the entrance. Some bank libraries, for example, are built without barriers between the library and its principal users.

If the library is to remain open at all times, an attempt must be made to see that what happens when the librarian is not present does not result in more work when the librarian returns. This can be accomplished by clearly spelling out procedures for library users to follow when the librarian is not present. One procedure that has to be very simple is the circulation routine. The overwhelming argument against the twenty-four-hour library is that materials disappear and there is no record of who has taken them. By educating library users about the need for circulation control, and by making it as easy as possible for them to record necessary borrowing information, the librarian will save significant amounts of time trying to track down lost items.

Another time-saving device can be the reshelving of materials used in the library by the library users, but this only saves time if the items are reshelved correctly. One cannot expect library users to be highly proficient at library tasks, nor greatly interested in performing them, but time spent by the librarian in educating and persuading users to follow certain procedures will save the librarian much more time later on. The use of signs is, of course, mandatory, but personal reminders and reinforcement are also usually required. In the very small public library, with its mixed population of users, it may not be possible or practical for library users to perform any of the librarian's functions.

If the problems associated with having the library open at times when the librarian is not present are insurmountable (and they may well be), some other arrangement must be made if users are to have access to information. One method is to leave the key to the library with the janitorial or security staff and have them assume responsibility for issuing the key to library users who must sign in and out when the library is closed. In spite of this safeguard, some problems are still likely to occur. Once an individual has opened the library, other users may wander in and out, so the need to provide clear instructions and adequate signs remains even with this method.

Current technology now makes it possible for the library to be accessible to anyone who has an embossed user's card or one with a bar code label which can be inserted in a device that records the user's name and the time he entered and left the library through an electronically controlled door. This is another alternative to consider if an "open door" policy proves ineffective. Any library will lose a few books over the course of a year and if the amount of loss is not excessive, such costs can be considered as part of the cost of "doing business."

The last thing the librarian should try to do is to hire someone to "babysit" the library during hours when the librarian is not there. A major goal of the very small library is to gain additional personnel and be allowed to grow. The librarian does want to hire someone, but not to perform such a passive function as merely keeping the library open. Additional personnel should improve library service for all users. This can best be accomplished, when feasible, by adding staff members who can play an active part in improving library operation.

Volunteers

In addition to other efforts to conserve the precious time of the librarian, there is at least one way that has proven effective for many libraries to actually increase the size of their staffs without spending additional funds. This method is the effective use of volunteers. Volunteers can be taught to perform a variety of library functions, and those who are motivated can be of great help to the librarian. Some of the negative factors associated with volunteer help have to do with lack of dependability, frequent turnover, and selective motivation for only certain types of library work. If volunteers are used they must be recruited, trained, supervised, and evaluated, and it is perhaps best for the librarian to consider volunteers as regular library staff with regard to any management problems that may arise.

In most libraries, the use of a volunteer program is probably worth investigating, particularly for the very small public library. Such a program can be initiated on a very limited basis and if successful, continued and improved as a means of conserving the librarian's time for other more demanding functions.

The source for volunteers will depend upon the type of small library. In a library for an art museum or an art school, a friends of the museum group may be a ready source. In the case of a hospital library, the institution may already have a volunteer program, such as an auxiliary group, that can be approached. In a for-profit organization such as an insurance agency, community job training agencies for young people or the underemployed may be a source for volunteers. Various other job training agencies associated with local government may be seeking temporary placements where on-the-job experience can be acquired. There is always the chance that someone is interested in being active in an organization or institution and is willing to contribute some time to the library. A notice in the organization's newsletter may reach friends and relatives of those already employed.

In selecting volunteers, one should consider skills needed by the library and the ability of the individual to work independently with a minimum of training. Typing and keyboarding skills are always useful. The ability to interact in a personable and effective manner with library users may be essential. Answering the telephone may have a high priority. Accuracy and attention to detail are critical for the consistency required in many library operations. The volunteer may represent the library to many of the users and should convey the image that the library hopes to project. Flexibility is important in a volunteer. Frequently volunteers are pleased to perform only certain tasks, but the librarian must determine what needs to be accomplished and use volunteers that can accommodate these needs. For these reasons, volunteers should be carefully interviewed before being accepted by the library.

If volunteers are to be an ongoing part of the library's operation, then an orientation and training manual probably should be developed to address recurring needs. This may save much of the librarian's time in the long run and provide a degree of consistency not otherwise possible.

Occasionally, the librarian in the very small library may be asked to accept a library school student intern. This is not a way for the librarian to get rid of some of the drudgery of library work. In fact, taking on an intern implies an educational commitment that will take a considerable amount of the librarian's time. The time spent meeting the educational needs of the intern will certainly exceed time saved with this additional staff member.

Use of other company employees

An alternative to the use of volunteers involves the use of other company employees based on some sort of formal agreement. The library should not be thought of as a dumping ground for problem employees of the organization or institution, but it may be useful to let other department managers know that the library can use help from other departments whenever they have slack periods or need to get someone out from under foot for a short period of time.

If employees can be convinced that the library serves the needs of all and aids in the success of the organization, they may be inclined to help the library directly through participation in library operations. It may even be possible for the understaffed library to initiate a program whereby certain individuals from each department, such as departmental secretaries or administrative assistants, are regularly scheduled at the library for brief work periods. This can help other departments in the organization by giving their employees insights into library use and by showing them how to take advantage of available information sources. This will provide the library with a steady stream of individuals who can be considered as additional staff members and can be assigned to perform certain library functions.

Of at least equal importance is the chance the librarian has to personally convert individuals in the organization into library users and library promoters. Ignorance of the true function of the library and the part the library plays or can play in achieving the larger organizational goals may be one of the greatest deterrents to effective library use and development.

Increasing staff size

An obvious means of overcoming a staff shortage is to convince the proper administrative authorities that more staff is needed, but this is often not a possibility. Therefore, the librarian must be creative and seek ways of achieving library objectives with little additional help. This must be accomplished without greatly cutting into the librarian's own time.

Any time-saving device should be considered by the librarian in performing library duties. The telephone, when properly used, can help the librarian. The use of an answering device attached to the telephone allows the librarian to be absent from the library. The telephone can also be used to provide a quicker and easier means of performing many library functions. For example, the retrieval of an overdue book, notification that material is waiting to be picked up, or a request for help on the evaluation of an item for possible acquisition can all be handled with a telephone call instead of devoting time to writing a memo or visiting an office.

No mention has been made in this chapter of the possibility of finding an outside source of funding for the employment of additional staff such as might be provided by a federal or state grant. Some possibilities do exist in this area, but the major problem is that additional staff leads to additional levels of service that do not disappear even when the grant support for the added position is no longer available.

One potential grant source to investigate is the state library. Most of the funds under federal programs are for the development of public libraries. However, some state libraries have promoted networks that include various types of libraries in one system. These library systems often include special libraries that become eligible for funding as part of a system. Other specialized programs may be available to individual types of very small libraries. Many small hospital libraries have come into existence or been improved through funds from the Medical Library Assistance Act. Some of these monies are also distributed at the local level through programs of the Regional Medical Library Program of the National Library of Medicine. Libraries supporting the humanities may qualify for support from the National Endowment for the Humanities. Private foundations can also be approached for library support. A number of directories list the purposes and programs of private foundations and appropriate individuals to contact. The librarian should become familiar with any foundations located in the same geographic area and approach these first if their interests are compatible with library needs.

For-profit organizations will seldom have the same opportunities for outside sources of funding as nonprofit libraries. Still, some benefactors may be courted with success. Preferable to a grant with its accompanying accounting, reporting, and other restrictions on use of funds is an outright gift of money to augment the library's budget. The enterprising librarian may identify a number of projects that are in need of funding and become an active fund raiser for the library. However, this takes time away from other functions that may be more directly related to the goals of the library.

Higher management needs to be convinced that the provision of library and information resources is a principal responsibility of the organization. Outside funding may be one way of augmenting these services, especially with regard to special needs, but the ongoing operation of the library and the development of the collection should be met through organizational resources.

Suggested Readings

Collins, S. M. "Determining Effective Staffing Levels in Special Libraries." *Special Libraries* 75 (October 1984): 283–91.

Goldstein, M. Z., and C. M. Sweeney. "Aptitude Requirements for Library Assistants in Special Libraries." *Special Libraries* 70 (September 1979): 373–76.

Heiberger, E. H. "Hiring During a Hiring Freeze: The Statistical Edge." *Bulletin of the Medical Library Association* 72 (October 1984): 393–94.

Landau, H. B. "Contract Services in the Special Library." *Special Libraries* 64 (April 1973): 175–80.

Matthews, P. J. "Finding the Fulcrum: Using Personal Time Management to Balance Career, Family, and Personal Interests." *Illinois Libraries* 69 (February 1987): 143–50.

Sandore, Beth, and Betsy Baker. "Changing Concepts of Motivation and Productivity in the Library." *Illinois Libraries* 69 (February 1987): 122–26.

5 Physical Characteristics of the Library

Most special libraries, particularly those with few employees, are very small, usually less than 3,000 square feet.[1] Making good use of such a small space is the subject of this chapter. We will concentrate on some of the principal features of any small library and how such limited size can be best utilized. Considerations include library location, shelving, user and work areas, and library access.

Library location

The physical placement of the library is a prime consideration in determining the extent to which the library will be used. A central location with easy access for the greatest number of potential users is the first preference for a location site. Principal user groups should have as direct access to the library as possible. If such placement is not possible, then the library's purposes would be best served by being located in some part of the organization where it can be given adequate space for its current needs and room for expansion.

If the library is not located on the first floor, then consideration must be given to receiving shipments of books and serials; access to elevators will be important. Locating the library near a facility such as a cafeteria could be an asset if the facility is widely used; however, if this is also a public facility, as is the case in many hospitals, the location of the library in such a high traffic area may result in excessive noise and unauthorized users entering the library.

Load-bearing capabilities

Any library location should be selected with the aid of those in charge of space management and the institution's engineering department. The number of library books and serials will usually grow as much as 10 to 13 percent annually, and the corresponding increase in weight is dramatic. The recommended load-bearing capability for the stack area of a library is 150 pounds per square foot.[2] If the library cannot be situated in a location that allows for the increasing weight of the collection, an alternative site will need to be selected. If no other space is available, the librarian and others involved in planning should consider other possibilities such as switching to microform storage, off-site storage of little used material, or a no-growth policy in which materials are removed every time new materials are added to the collection.

Lighting

Natural lighting is not a requirement for the library, however, windows have aesthetic value, and most library users prefer them. Natural lighting, if available, should be utilized to the best possible advantage. Windows should not be blocked by the placement of shelves or stacks. Consideration should be given to the possible deleterious effect of direct sunlight upon library materials, and appropriate measures should be taken to make sure that natural light is utilized without unwanted side effects for either users or materials.

Generally, heavily used areas will require greater candlepower than some of the lesser used areas.[3] The stacks are usually not as well lighted, but it is hard to decipher classification numbers on bottom shelves if sufficient lighting is not provided.

Work areas, such as one for technical processing, should have the same amount of light as user areas but they should be on separate circuits if possible, so that lights can be turned off when these areas are not in use.

Shelving

Shelving for monographs and serials usually involves several different approaches. The main collection is most frequently kept in "ranges" made up of shelving sections with five shelves each. Each shelf can house approximately eight books per linear foot. Accordingly, each three-foot shelf could hold approximately twenty-five books when full. However, shelves should be no more than two-thirds full to allow room for reshelving and collection growth. A range is composed of a number of five-shelf units, and is usually double-faced with shelves on two sides. The number of double-faced units within the range is variable, but in the very small library the collection is not likely to be so large that breaks for aisles will be required. Five-shelf units can usually be expanded to hold seven shelves, but problems of reaching the top shelf and difficulty in seeing call numbers on the bottom shelf make the use of five shelves more acceptable. Shelving should be standard, adjustable, and suitable for both monograph and serial collections.

Current unbound periodical issues will require a different type of shelving for maximum utilization and appropriate display. Most current periodical areas utilize some type of slanting shelves upon which the latest issue can be placed vertically with the full cover displayed. Earlier issues in volumes are stored under the slanting shelf, which pivots out, or they are placed below on flat shelves. Such display shelves do not make the maximum economy of shelving space and may not be practical for the very small library. Other alternatives would include housing current issues along with earlier volumes in the regular stack area. For recent issues, or other unbound issues, one should use cut-corner file cases or so-called Princeton files to hold loose issues. This makes shelving on conventional library shelves more practical. Another approach would be to display on slanting shelves or in an upright display rack only the most recently received issues of the most heavily used journals. Earlier issues of the same volume would be kept in the stacks. The librarian may want to arrange a few of the more important recent journals on a table for browsing. For example, journals received on any one day might be displayed until being replaced by the next day's arrivals. If it is not possible to display recent journal issues then a typed list of the journals checked in each day could be made available to library users. However, in the very small library, it may be difficult to find staff time to provide even this service.

Counter-high shelving is ideal for housing a ready reference collection as well as for shelving abstracting and indexing services. Conventional high shelves are usually double-faced so that materials can be shelved on both sides. Counter-high shelves may also allow for shelving on both sides. Most shelving of this type is custom-made and approximately forty inches in height so that the top can be used as a counter on which to consult the reference sources. Counter-high shelving can also be used as a method of dividing areas between staff and user spaces.

Special shelving and housing arrangements may be required for other types of library materials. For example, maps will require cases if they are to be fully protected and easily accessible to users. Vertical files are useful for pamphlets and other materials that do not require classification and would not stand on more traditional shelving. Photographs and other audiovisual materials may also require special housing and/or special containers.

Pullout shelves or flat shelves can also be installed among the standard journal and monograph shelves. These provide a working surface for those using materials in the stacks.

Whatever arrangements are made, shelving should be functional, make the most effective use of available space, and meet the aesthetic needs of both the librarian and library users. Shelving must protect the collection and provide ease for those who have to withdraw and replace materials in their original shelf locations.

User areas

User space can be an important determinant of whether or not a library will be effectively used. Ideally, there should be sufficient user space located adjacent to the materials patrons will be using. When space for the collection is extremely limited, user space may need to be reduced or even eliminated. If users are in close proximity to the library and have offices to which they can take library materials, this may not prove too great an inconvenience. If such is the case, circulation policies will have to be formulated to aid users in obtaining the materials they need. In addition, sufficient photocopy facilities will take some of the pressure off the library to provide more seating. Even when a library provides sufficient user space, many patrons will still prefer to use library materials in their own offices or homes.

The space for users need not be all in one area; there can be small amounts of user space scattered throughout the library. With strategic placement of a few individual carrels, users may be able to find a place to sit down in virtually any part of the library. It is important to remember when setting up areas that the use of some types of materials requires more space than others. The map collection, for example, is easiest to use at fairly large tables. Many librarians place easy chairs in the current periodical display area to encourage browsing of the new journals received. If the library has a terminal for online database searching, a place should be provided for the search requester to sit while the search is being performed.

In most small libraries there is no need to seat a large number of users at any one time. One exception might be the very small public library, where periods of heavy student use can be anticipated. For most small libraries, even those heavily used as in hospitals and business firms, a small amount of user space is usually sufficient because not everyone comes to the library at the same time.

Work areas

Technical processing

Technical processing is a library function that can and should be isolated from public areas. The processing area should have large work surfaces with sufficient shelves and cupboards to hold supplies and materials to be processed. A sink is also desirable. Users should not have free access to this area because many of the materials being processed will not yet be adequately identified as library property. Any materials taken from this area prior to the completion of processing should first pass through the hands of the librarian.

Standards for libraries advise individual work stations of no less than 125 square feet,[4] but in the very small library, the librarian will often be performing the processing alone and can fit the necessary materials into space that does not seem suitable for other needs. A converted closet or some other area detached from the library proper may serve as a suitable processing area. It is not recommended that the librarian try to perform public service functions and technical processing operations at the same time.

The librarian's office

In a very small library with limited space for necessary library functions, it is worth questioning whether a separate office for the librarian is really necessary. The answer to this will depend to a great extent on how the librarian views his or her position. If the librarian acknowledges the importance of the management functions (planning, organizing, direction, controlling), then an office in which to perform these functions and to escape from the pressure of daily operations will seem essential. Files pertaining to the library's operation need to be protected in a secure area and these can best be housed in the librarian's office. Private conferences with library users and others will require some place within the library with a degree of privacy. Private space is important, and for someone who is responsible for all library operations it may be critical. Even very limited personal space for the librarian should be considered essential in planning the library.

Library access

Many library users may find little time or need to visit the library in person. In the library of the future, one mediated by electronics, users may never need to come to the library. Instead, micro-computers connected to library files will be used to deposit needed information at terminals located in users' offices, laboratories, and homes. Currently, however, the library is still in a good position to provide for the needs of remote users. Telephone requests for specific materials or library services such as literature searches should be encouraged by the librarian of the small library. The problems often associated with performing an adequate user interview to determine "real" information needs are not solved only through a face-to-face interview. The problems are usually semantic or reflect a rigidness that prevents effective communication from taking place.

In a busy operation, the librarian may be trying to serve a number of users within the library and find that the telephone is a constant interruption. Under these conditions, a telephone answering machine to record information requests and messages may be highly useful and enable the librarian to manage his or her time more effectively.

One should avoid receiving information requests through a third party if at all possible. A user may ask that a secretary contact the library and request a literature search. The librarian is definitely at a disadvantage under such circumstances and may not be able to respond at all, depending upon how well the secretary understands what is really needed. The telephone provides the means necessary for an interactive user interview and, if used effectively, often makes remote library access desirable.

Users may also send memos and other communications to the library to request specific materials such as reprints of particular articles, and on occasion, literature searches. Lack of information may make it necessary for the librarian to then telephone the user. This extra step can be avoided if users are trained to provide essential information: name and position of caller; location; a detailed statement of information needed, including the reason for the request (for literature searches); form in which the answer is to be provided; time within which the information or item is needed; what is already known about the subject, such as the user's source of information relating to the request; and limitations as to language, format, or amount of information needed.

When responding to remote users' needs, the same criteria that apply to in-house users should be employed to establish the priority for processing each information request.

After-hours access

Some of the means of controlling after-hours library access were discussed in chapter 4. This section offers advice on dealing with some of the problems created by allowing library access when the librarian is not present. It is reasonable to expect, for example, that a corporate library, an engineering library, or a hospital library be available at times when information is needed but the library is not normally open. In any type of organization where the employees are a well-defined group and some type of facility security is provided, allowing access to the library when the librarian is not present should not be a matter for great concern.

Many librarians are reluctant to provide after-hours access because they often find the library in a state of disarray the next morning. Frequently, materials have been removed from the library without any checkout record. The problem of disarray is probably inescapable to a large extent, but appropriate signs explaining the rules of the library should be posted so that users know they apply whether the librarian is there or not. For example, if food and drink are not allowed in the library, then users should respect these rules even if the librarian is not present. Those who break rules after hours may need to be personally reminded of them by the librarian.

As for the records required to keep track of library materials, a simple circulation system will be the best means of ensuring compliance. If need be, a sheet for names can be provided at the door; anyone leaving with library materials would then be reminded that they need to place their names on the list. The next day that the library is open, the librarian can call the individual and find out what materials have been taken from the library. This is probably the simplest system, but it requires more of the librarian's time. A better system would be one in which users identified materials taken from the library regardless of whether the librarian is present or not. A self-charging system that is in place even when the librarian is present saves the librarian's time and may train users to always check out materials whenever they use the library. However, any such system usually seems to break down "after hours," so the librarian must be prepared to take appropriate steps to make sure that adequate records are somehow provided.

Prevention of serious problems is largely a matter of public relations and of the general feeling of morale and loyalty within the organization. This will be reflected in the way that users treat library materials. If there is a trend toward indifference or vandalism throughout the organization, the library will not escape it.

Signs

It has been said that a sign is a silent librarian.[5] One cannot argue with this as long as one also considers the public relations value in the design of such signs. Informative signs that direct the flow of traffic in a library can be highly useful to users who "hate to ask" and to librarians who feel that all they do is respond to directional questions. In addition, signs that can be placed in appropriate locations during times when the library is not normally staffed may make the library easier to use. As a general rule, signs should be used sparingly. They should be limited to a few informational facts and should not be done in a "cutesy" manner. They should convey the professional image of the library. One sign that must be designed with considerable care is the one outside the library. Too often this is an inexpensive, small sign produced in-house with a minimum of time and effort. The sign announcing the library creates the first impression of the library, and it should attempt to convey the image the librarian hopes to achieve for the library. Just because this is a very small library does not mean that it is not providing a highly important and extensive service.

Morale

It should be noted that the morale of library staff and the resulting level of productivity may be closely related to the quality of work space within the library. This closely parallels the theory that conditions such as satisfactory work space serve as hygienic or environmental factors that may promote job dissatisfaction, but do not promote job satisfaction.[6] Accordingly, work space probably affects productivity. This may not be a primary consideration for the very small library with only one employee, but unsatisfactory library space may affect the productivity of library users. The use of what Ambrose[7] calls sociophysical analysis might lead to improved library effectiveness.

Notes

1. This would be a room approximately 50' by 60' and is considered a generous estimate based on a random sample of libraries reporting staff of only one person from the work by A. M. Rees and Susan Crawford, *Directory of Health Sciences Libraries in the U.S.* (Cleveland: Case Western Reserve University, 1979), and the one by B. T. Darnay, ed., *Directory of Special Libraries and Information Centers*, 9th ed. (Detroit: Gale Research Co., 1985). Holdings for such libraries consistently number less than 5,000 volumes and, in many instances, less than 1,000 volumes. Housing for such numbers could easily be achieved within these space limits. A general space calculation of 120 square feet per user is presented on page 269 of the work by Janet Bradley, ed., *Hospital Library Management* (Chicago: Medical Library Association, 1983). A library of 3,000 square feet could accommodate twenty-five users and provide necessary room for the collection and other library functions. According to figures in J. L. Ahrensfeld et al., eds., *Special Libraries: A*

Guide for Management, 2nd rev. ed. (Washington, D.C.: Special Libraries Association, 1986), a small library may require only 2,000 square feet while a large library might exceed 10,000 square feet (p. 46).

2. Special Libraries Association, "Objectives and Standards for Special Libraries," *Special Libraries* 21 (December 1964): 671–80. See also R. A. Fraley, and C. L. Anderson, *Library Space Planning* (New York: Neal-Schuman Publishers, 1985, pp. 44–45.

3. See Special Libraries Association, "Objectives and Standards for Special Libraries," *Special Libraries* 21 (December 1964): 680, J. L. Ahrensfeld et. al., eds., *Special Libraries: A Guide for Management,* 2d rev. ed. (Washington, D.C.: Special Libraries), p. 48 Janet Bradley, ed.; and *Hospital Library Management* (Chicago: Medical Library Association, 1983), p. 286.

4. Special Libraries Association, "Objectives and Standards for Special Libraries," *Special Libraries* 21 (December 1964): 680.

5. Rita Kohn, and Krysta Tepper, *You Can Do It: A PR Skills Manual for Librarians* (Metuchen, N.J.: Scarecrow Press, 1981), p. 62.

6. R. D. Stueart and B. B. Moran, *Library Management,* 3d ed. (Littleton, Colo.: Libraries Unlimited, 1987), pp. 140–42.

7. Karen Ambrose and L. Ambrose, "Improving Library Effectiveness Through Sociophysical Analysis," *Bulletin of the Medical Library Association* 65 (October 1977): 438–42.

Cited Literature

Ahrensfeld, J. L. et al., eds. *Special Libraries: A Guide for Management.* 2d rev. ed. Washington, D.C.: Special Libraries Association, 1986.

Ambrose, K., and L. Ambrose. "Improving Library Effectiveness Through Sociophysical Analysis." *Bulletin of the Medical Library Association* 65 (October 1977): 438–42.

Bradley, Janet, ed. *Hospital Library Management.* Chicago: Medical Library Association, 1983.

Darnay, B. T., ed. *Directory of Special Libraries and Information Centers.* 9th ed. Detroit: Gale Research Co., 1985.

Fraley, R. A., and C. L. Anderson. *Library Space Planning.* New York: Neal-Schuman Publishers, 1985.

Isacco, J. M. "Work Spaces, Satisfaction, and Productivity in Libraries." *Library Journal* (May 1, 1985): 27–30.

Kohn, Rita, and Krysta Tepper. *You Can Do It: A PR Skills Manual for Librarians.* Metuchen, N.J.: Scarecrow Press, 1981.

Rees, A. M., and Susan Crawford. *Directory of Health Sciences Libraries in the U.S.* Cleveland: Case Western Reserve University, 1979.

Special Libraries Association. "Objectives and Standards for Special Libraries." *Special Libraries* 21 (December 1964): 671–80.

Stueart, R. D., and B. B. Moran. *Library Management.* 3d ed. Littleton, Colo.: Libraries Unlimited, 1987.

Suggested Readings

Brand, Marvine, ed. *Security for Libraries: People, Buildings, Collections.* Chicago: American Library Association, 1984.

Bube, J. L. "The Ergonomics/Human Factors Approach to Health Sciences Libraries." *Bulletin of the Medical Library Association* 73 (July 1985): 254–58.

Dahlgren, A. C. "Effective Space Utilization With Whatcha Got." *Iowa Library Quarterly* 22 (1985): 3–18.

Esterquest, R. T. "Shelving Medical Serials for Reader Convenience." *Bulletin Medical Library Association* 48 (1960): 175–83.

Fraley, R. A., and C. L. Anderson. *Library Space Planning.* New York: Neal-Schuman Publishers, 1985.

Hubbard, W. J. *Stack Management: A Practical Guide to Shelving and Maintaining Library Collections.* Chicago: American Library Association, 1981.

Hyman, Richard J. *Shelf Access in Libraries.* Chicago: American Library Association, 1982.

Kohl, D. F. *Administration, Personnel, Buildings and Equipment: A Handbook for Library Management.* Santa Barbara: ABC-Clio Information Services, 1985.

Lushington, Nolan, and N. M. Willis, Jr. *Libraries Designed for Users.* Syracuse: Gaylord Professional Publications, 1979.

Mason, Ellsworth. *Mason on Library Buildings.* Metuchen, N.J.: Scarecrow Press, 1980.

Metcalf, K. D. et al. *Planning Academic and Research Library Buildings.* Rev. ed. Chicago: American Library Association, 1986.

Rovelstad, Howard. "Guidelines for Planning Facilities for Sci-tech Libraries." *Science & Technology Libraries* 3 (Summer 1983): 3–20.

Watterson, R. M. "Shelving Current Journals: Another Approach." *Bulletin of the Medical Library Association* 58 (April 1970): 191–93.

6 Acquiring and Developing the Collection

Public libraries make up the bulk of very small libraries in this country, but special libraries also comprise a large percentage in this size range. In addition to monographs and serials, which are the mainstay of virtually all libraries, there is often a need for special libraries to acquire technical reports, patents, government documents, maps, photographs, and other assorted materials. In some cases these materials will be in non-print formats such as audio and visual packages; in other cases they may be available on microfilm and microfiche. More recently, digital formats (electronically coded) are becoming commonplace.

The principal objective of the librarian is to acquire needed materials, regardless of format, as quickly as possible and with the least expenditure of effort. The librarian should seek to eliminate the need to write an abundance of correspondence, check invoices extensively, or spend time filing multiple forms. The librarian in the very small library should look for quick and easy ways to consolidate many of the selection and acquisition processes. This chapter will examine some of the requirements needed for building an up-to-date, representative collection designed to meet the needs of a specific group of users. As with other aspects of library management, the objective is to achieve the goals of collection development while economizing on the amount of time that such activities require.

Building a collection involves two functions: the selection of material, and the acquisition of that material. In order for a small collection (one that does not have research potential requiring permanent retention) to remain vital and reflective of its users' needs, less useful material must be removed from the collection as new material is added. Therefore, "weeding" (the removal of materials no longer needed) will also be discussed.

The collection development policy

A collection development policy (CDP) is a necessity for any library. It provides a framework within which to define the boundaries of the collection and it serves as a guide to anyone involved in selecting material for the library. Accordingly, the more specific the parameters of the CDP, the easier it is for someone to follow previous practices used in building a collection tailored to meet the needs of a given group of users.

The collection development policy should specify the scope and depth of the collection. Scope refers to the breadth of subjects to be represented in the collection, and depth refers to the degree to which those subjects are to be represented. Different formats (books, journals, newspapers, and audiovisuals, etc.) to be collected should be identified; foreign languages to be included and levels of collection development should also be described. Levels of collection development can be described as comprehensive, research, study, basic, or minimal. The levels may vary depending on the subject area. A number of writers including Conway, Eakin, and Perkins address the topic of different levels of collection development. The CDP should also include a weeding policy for the collection that specifies the frequency of performance along with the criteria to be employed for removing material.

It is often helpful to include a well-defined gift policy in the CDP. Even the very small library may find that it is inundated with gifts of materials from users. Such gifts may be forthcoming for a variety of reasons. Whenever possible, the final disposition of all gifts should be in the hands of the librarian, and the decision about what to retain should be made quickly. No stipulations should be allowed as part of a gift unless there are overwhelming reasons for accepting such restrictions. Please refer to the end of this chapter for an outline of a sample collection development policy.

Selection of materials

The selection process will largely depend upon the librarian's identifying needed materials through notices in the journal litera-ture, and from advertising flyers that cross her desk. The collection development policy should guide the librarian with regard to sub-ject viability and whether an item is needed in light of material al-ready in the collection. Once the collection development policy has been written, the librarian of a newly created library can begin a collection by consulting core lists of available material. These are lists of materials that should be considered for purchase in building an initial library collection. There are many such lists in medicine, but probably the best known is the Brandon and Hill list of selected books and journals for the small medical library. This publication is revised every two years and aids in identifying items for first purchase if funds are limited. Some examples of core lists are given in the references for this chapter. A useful introduction to the selection and acquisition of specialized materials can be found in the somewhat dated monograph by Kaiser that provides a detailed bibliography with some useful references. Other sources for specialized materials are in literature guides for specific dis-ciplines.

When deciding whether or not to add certain items, one must also consider the amount of money available in the budget for the purchase of all types of materials and the amount of space within the library for new material. The acquisitions budget should usually be expended throughout the entire year so that new materials may be acquired as they appear. In some instances the librarian could easily spend the entire materials budget in the first three months of the year, but materials published after that time might be lost forever as they go out of print before the librarian has a new budget to work with.

The selection of periodicals is often subject to restrictions as well. If shelf space for periodicals is at a premium, a librarian might pass up a subscription to a new journal in a field already covered by other journals in the collection. For many libraries, a subscrip-tion to a particular journal is a commitment by the library to pur-chase, support, and house that periodical forever (barring a change in the character of the library's collection). Such a commitment means that space reserved for the future housing of that journal may be substantial even though the initial subscription may only require a small amount of space. The library's users should be con-sulted whenever possible to aid in this selection process.

Ideally, the librarian might prefer to have all selection of materials done by users of the library. However, interest in selection varies considerably from user to user, and without the librarian to oversee the process, response to only the more vocal and interested individuals would result in an unbalanced collection. It is the librarian's responsibility to see that all subjects are represented in accordance with the collection development policy. Still, one should try to involve users in the selection process to the extent possible. Request forms for the purchase of materials should be readily available within the library and, if possible, at the department or unit level within the organization. Each individual in the organization could be given his or her own supply if this is feasible.

Another way of involving others is to have a library committee of users as liaisons for their units. The selection function should not be transferred to this committee, since the librarian is responsible for the overall development of the collection and for the expenditure of funds. However, the committee can advise the librarian, and each member can contribute suggestions in his or her area of expertise.

Advertisements and publishers' announcements should be routed to library users for their evaluations. Ideally, users will be moved to fill out a "request for purchase" slip if they spot an item that is important and should be added to the collection. Since their time is as important as the librarian's, a simple check-off scheme may be the best way to motivate users to return their suggestions to the librarian. Some materials go out of print rather quickly, so users should be reminded to review these announcements in a timely fashion.

A librarian with the necessary subject expertise could conceivably be the only individual involved in the selection process, but this is not advisable. The librarian should build a system that ensures the collection's development within the prescribed boundaries of the collection development policy. Any group of users that is actively involved in building the collection will be more likely to utilize the library and support its activities. A major purchase involving a substantial amount of money (a multivolume work, for example) should probably be supported by advice from the users. Expensive sets may carry all the marks of authority, but if they are not used, they have not only drawn funds from the acquisitions budget, they have also earmarked significant shelf space for the future.

Approval plans

An approval plan, in which the library automatically receives materials that match a prearranged subject and format profile, is not very useful for the small library with a limited budget. Approval plan dealers are reluctant to go to the expense of setting up and operating such a plan unless a substantial amount will be spent annually. If the library budget is large, and the librarian can use an approval plan effectively, then the librarian can save considerable time. More importantly, an approval plan allows for selection with the material in hand and makes it that much easier to involve library users in the selection process. The librarian may choose to send potential acquisitions to users with an evaluation form, or display the materials for a limited number of days in a central location. In any event, the process must not abdicate the librarian's responsibility for selection to a third party.

Approval plans must have "return privileges," and these should be used by the librarian to ensure that the collection develops along predetermined CDP guidelines. Usually a return rate of less than 10 percent indicates that the library's profile is too narrow and that some wanted materials are probably being missed. A return rate of more than 20 percent may mean that the profile is too broad and that the librarian is spending needless time looking at materials that should not have been sent in the first place.

Acquisition of materials

Acquisitions is the part of library operation that is involved with identifying a source from which to acquire needed material, gathering sufficient bibliographic information to order the material, receiving the material, and clearing and filing all of the paperwork for each transaction.

Acquisition procedures have a way of eating up large amounts of a librarian's time, and in the very small library, these operations should not be allowed to detract unduly from time needed to provide user services. Such procedures should begin as the selection process begins, and the two (selection and acquisition) should compliment each other so that information gathered during the selection phase can be utilized with as little change as possible during the acquisition process.

Information from user request forms and from other sources announcing available material will usually need some verification before it can be used on a purchase order. Accuracy in gathering initial data is highly important. When the time comes to issue a purchase order, one should not have to recheck data or look for an element that should have been noted when the request was first examined. Of greatest importance are elements that uniquely identify the item being ordered, such as the International Standard Book Number (ISBN) or International Standard Serials Number, which is now usually available in any complete bibliographic description including publishers' announcements and bibliographic listings in journals.

Standing orders

The use of standing orders is a principal way of saving the librarian's time in the acquisition process. As the name implies, when an item is on standing order, the library will continue to receive the item until that order is canceled. These orders usually apply to materials that are intended to be published on a continuing schedule, and this ordering system guarantees that items always wanted for the collection will not be missed. Standing orders may be used for annuals, new editions, volumes in sets, or other continuing publication patterns. The disadvantages are that in most cases standing orders do not carry return privileges and often must be initiated separately with each publisher. The librarian will need a "tickler" (reminder) file to help guarantee that items on standing order are received when they become available.

Vendors and discounts

Selection of a vendor is highly important to the librarian of the very small library because direct ordering is usually more expensive than the use of a vendor. Vendors operate in different fashions, and the services they provide may be greatly influenced by the method of operation. A vendor who specializes in materials by type or subject matter may be more suitable for certain acquisitions. For example, a vendor of government publications might be the best source for that format while a vendor of medical materials may have access to the works of most major medical publishers.

Because of the high cost of holding inventories, some vendors will seek out requested materials rather than attempting to have a large stock of books on hand at all times. This approach may reduce one of the most beneficial services to the librarian—speed in delivery. Other vendors may have a substantial number of books on hand but offer little or no discount because of higher operating costs. When selecting a vendor, one should consult colleagues in similar types of libraries. Unfortunately, if centralized bidding procedures are required, the low bidder is likely to be the vendor who offers the highest discount but also the least amount of service. For the very small library, service at the expense of a few dollars may be money well spent.

Every librarian will want to order some materials directly from the publisher. This does take up time, but in some cases publishers are the only source for such materials. At times the amount of discount available through direct ordering will make this an attractive alternative. The secret is to order direct selectively and find a vendor who is able to supply most wanted materials quickly and with a discount when possible. Changing to a new vendor is not as much of a problem with monographs as it is with serials. If a vendor is not living up to expectations, look for one whose performance may be better.

Publisher discounts vary and are frequently referred to as "long" or "short" discounts. According to Kronick and Bowden, most health sciences publishers offer short discounts in the range of 10 to 18 percent to vendors, who then pass on a lesser discount to libraries. Long discount items are usually nontechnical books such as those purchased by a public library. In this case, the publisher can expect to sell several thousand copies. Long discounts may range as high as 40 to 45 percent with the higher figure for multiple copy purchases. Because of the relatively small discount available on specialized materials, many small libraries may be well justified in placing as many orders as possible with a vendor who specializes in providing complete orders as quickly as possible. Many vendors will make an extra effort to find needed materials even though they may not be part of the vendor's inventory.

Acquisition files

A key to efficient and effective acquisition work is the maintenance of files. The fewer files the better, but there are a number of elements that the librarian must be able to trace at any given time in the acquisitions process. The use of an NCR (no carbon required) multipart order form will facilitate the keeping of manual files. One copy of the order form will go to the publisher or vendor, a second will be placed in the public catalog (card catalog) under the author or another suitable entry, a third is for the "on order" file to prevent duplication of orders, and a fourth can be placed in a file to be used in generating cards for the catalog or an online electronic record. Depending upon the type of operation envisioned, the latter file might also serve as a notification file used to tell users about the outcome of their requests for materials. Whether or not the librarian chooses to purchase materials that have been recommended by users, each person submitting a purchase request form should be notified as soon as possible of the outcome of that request.

Receiving materials

Once materials are received, shipments need to be checked for completeness and for physical condition. A brief collation (page by page examination) of materials may identify those that are in unacceptable condition. Do not hesitate to request a replacement copy for any imperfect materials, but do not send the imperfect materials back until you are asked to do so. Often the publisher will request that you destroy an imperfect copy rather than return it.

Judgment must be your guide as you determine how to deal with incomplete orders. In some cases, the supplier will cancel orders for titles that are presently unavailable; in other cases an attempt will be made to complete the order whenever possible. From the librarian's standpoint, it is best to close each transaction as soon as possible so that one does not have to go back repeatedly to check on the same purchases. The librarian in the very small library should choose the approach that takes the least amount of time and generates the least amount of correspondence.

Record keeping

The librarian must be responsible for record keeping with regard to the materials budget. Such record keeping, along with purchasing, is usually centralized within any organization. In virtually all cases, however, the purchase of library materials (books, journals, audiovisuals, etc.) needs to be left in the hands of the librarian, for this is not equivalent to buying chairs, typewriters, and supplies. Once centralized purchasing department heads come to realize the need for the library to control its own materials purchasing and the library has established credibility, then such autonomy is usually a benefit to both the organization and the library. Even though the business office may keep track of library expenses, the librarian must also maintain records to ensure that accounts are not overspent and that the central system is not in error. Anyone charged with fiscal responsibility for funds should be concerned with keeping accurate records as to the expenditure of those funds. Centralized systems are prone to mistakes just as are other segments of the organization. Dual records provide the librarian with a check on the centralized records and, more importantly, provide up-to-date, daily information regarding unspent and unencumbered balances in the library materials accounts.

Serials

The acquisition of serials is usually better handled through a serials jobber. The subscription list for the library may often be handled in its entirety by the jobber who places subscriptions, pursues claims submitted by the library, and issues a single invoice to cover the cost of all subscriptions. The principal value of this approach is that the librarian is free to do other things. In exchange, the librarian must be willing to pay a small service change. A charge of 2 percent is frequently encountered. If there are many serial titles on a library's subscription list, this is money well spent, particularly for the very small library.

The trend throughout the publishing and distributing industry for library materials parallels the rapid adoption of automation that is taking place in libraries. Jobbers and others are offering automatic order systems in which the order information is transferred electronically between jobber and librarian. Record-keeping systems may also be offered and maintained by distributors as a service and a means of attracting and retaining library customers. The small library in particular may benefit from these services. In lieu of establishing its own automated integrated library system,[1] a small library may elect to access an automated system provided by a vendor or service bureau. If existing systems can be accessed effectively, then the savings in time to the librarian may be well worth the cost of subscribing to a vendor's automated services.

Audiovisual acquisitions

Audiovisuals present unique problems in selection and acquisition. One problem is the diversity of formats for some types of media. Videocassettes may be three-quarter-inch or the increasingly popular one-half-inch. Audio products may vary from reel tapes to cassettes. All types of media require appropriate hardware in order to be used. With limited budgets, small libraries must try to select machines that will accommodate a variety of format variations if possible. Bibliographic control of audiovisual materials as a means of identifying available materials is not as well organized as it is for books and journals. Some progress is being made, as in the Cataloging in Publication project of medically related audiovisuals through the National Library of Medicine. Another problem is that audiovisual materials usually cost quite a bit more than printed matter. For this reason, and because of variations in quality, preview prior to purchase is considered to be advantageous whenever possible. Library users should be part of the selection process to provide subject expertise in evaluating materials. Now that more and more audiovisual materials are being linked to microcomputers, increased emphasis on expenditures in this area of library operations can be anticipated.

Deposit accounts

Deposit accounts are required by a number of distributors or producers of information, resources, and services, including some government agencies such as the National Technical Information Service (NTIS), a major distributor of government documents along with the Superintendent of Documents. These accounts require that a library deposit funds in advance against future orders. The initial amount varies: NTIS requires a deposit of $25[2] while Bernan Associates (a jobber for U.S. documents) requires $50.[3] It is usually important that billings not exceed the deposit or the account may have to be reestablished causing a delay in service. Deposit accounts may be required, but libraries with budget restrictions should be sure that funds do not sit in such accounts indefinitely when they should be retrieved and spent elsewhere before the end of the fiscal year. One should keep the amount in deposit accounts as near as possible to the amount that will actually be required during the year.

Weeding

The weeding process ensures that the materials on the library's shelves are those most important in meeting the information needs of the library's users. For this reason, weeding (at times referred to as "deselection") should be an ongoing process and over the course of time, the entire collection should come under scrutiny.

Weeding should be done on a continuing basis, for some crowded libraries may find that a new acquisition cannot be added to the shelves unless an older or little used volume is removed. If the librarian finds that the weeding objective is not being achieved, then a periodic weeding schedule should be established and adhered to. Depending on how much space is available, weeding can be scheduled anywhere from every three months to once a year. Other reasons for weeding might also dictate the frequency needed. Materials that are badly damaged should either be repaired, replaced, or withdrawn from the collection. In some libraries, it may be necessary to remove inaccurate or outdated information from the collection to prevent its use by library patrons. Eakin suggests weeding multiple copies, outdated handbooks, manuals, review books, and books in poor condition. One should consider the availability of other editions and sources for the same information that may exist elsewhere in the collection. If the librarian is in doubt as to the value of a work being considered for discard, it may be helpful to check standard bibliographies or a list of historical materials. The health sciences librarian, for example, can refer to the Garrison and Morton bibliography.

If the library has an automated circulation system, it should be easy to identify materials that have limited or no circulation activity as candidates for weeding. In an active circulating collection, most materials should be checked out at some time over a two to three year period. However, in an archival collection, some needed works may never circulate. In many circulation systems, the use of a stamped date due slip in each book can serve as a record of its use. However, the librarian may have to examine each book in the collection in order to identify those that have not circulated. Electronic circulation systems may be able to provide such information with little effort. A number of readings on weeding are listed at the end of this chapter.

Processing acquisitions

Materials received by the library must be processed before they are ready for shelving. In addition to cataloging (discussed in the next chapter), they must receive ownership marks and have pockets and date due slips attached if these are to be used. The entire acquisitions process from ordering to shelf preparation can be provided by sources outside the library if the librarian so chooses. One method is to employ the services of a vendor who processes materials prior to shipping them to the ordering library. This method usually includes classification and cataloging, and catalog cards accompany the books in each shipment. The library will have to pay for this service, but it can usually be tailored to meet local needs while saving the time of the librarian.

A second approach might be to contract such services to another local library. As savings achieved through technology coincide with more or less fixed acquisition budgets for larger libraries, the size of technical service departments in many of the larger libraries will tend to decrease. One way for these larger libraries to keep technical service operations near their current size is by contracting to do processing for other libraries in the same geographic areas. Thus, the very small library might submit all orders for materials to a local university that would process the orders and send them on, receive the materials, process them to the library's specifications, invoice the library, and pay a middleman for the materials received. Such a service might be on a contract basis or a per title fee. The complex and efficient operating system of the university library would be available to the smaller library, and this might be extended to include the checking in of serials as well as other technical processing functions. The librarian of the small library should investigate both of these alternatives as a means of saving time and money.

Acquisition alternatives

Although document delivery and interlibrary loans (ILL) are services that augment the formal acquisitions program of the library, any materials that are needed frequently are not candidates for the ILL system. Rather, they are items that should be purchased. However, with more and more library budgets limited to no growth or increasing only slightly, libraries will have to seek access to materials outside their own collections with greater frequency than in the past. Libraries have traditionally attempted to provide collection-based services. This means that the bulk of materials needed by a library's users are acquired and added to that library's collection. As the need for information increases and budgets remain static, libraries are unable to provide collections that meet all needs and must therefore provide access-based services. Interlibrary loan and document delivery are access-based services that borrow or obtain photocopies of needed materials from other libraries or document vendors. These materials are not acquired for permanent addition to the library's collection.

It seems that this shift from collection-based to access-based services will increase for all libraries in the years ahead as cooperative collection development programs become widespread. In addition to accelerating costs for materials, small libraries with limited space will need to consider very carefully which materials actually need to be housed within the library and which are to be readily available by access from other libraries and vendors providing document delivery services.

One alternative that may prove to be advantageous for small libraries is the cooperative collection development program. In such a program, several small libraries within a geographic area may agree to purchase books and journals on a cooperative basis. This means that while some items may be acquired by all the cooperating libraries, only certain libraries would be required by agreement to acquire infrequently used materials. Other libraries would then borrow these materials as the need arose. In this fashion, several libraries can use their combined acquisitions budgets to cover a wider spectrum of the literature and still have access to available materials if and when they are needed.

A different approach that might be used with serials is to move from having the library subscribe to a journal that is infrequently used, to the purchase of individual copies of needed articles from that journal when they are requested by library users. A number of private document delivery services are now available from online vendors[4] and from information companies throughout the world. By using such services, libraries can provide needed articles without the commitment to purchase and house a particular journal.

The difference in price between library subscriptions and personal subscriptions for journals is one of the current problems facing many libraries. The fact that libraries are charged significantly larger amounts for journals may further encourage cooperative acquisition programs and a move toward the use of documents provided by vendors as an alternative to the very expensive practice of library journal subscription.

Of concern for any library in the move to access-based services is the matter of copyright. Currently libraries are burdened with extensive record-keeping systems to ensure that they are in compliance with copyright laws and guidelines. Access to documents through commercial vendors eliminates such record keeping. It is the vendor's responsibility to make sure that copyright holders are sufficiently compensated for the documents that are supplied to a vendor's customers. Librarians should generally be concerned that copyright holders make sufficient profit to ensure their continued existence and ability to provide information products.

In the not too distant future, full-text database systems, high speed printers, advanced graphic reproduction, and a change to a philosophy of access-based services will greatly alter the appearance and performance of many very small libraries. Because of telecommunication capabilities, it will no longer be necessary for a library to subscribe to and house any current journal; instead, there will be electronic access to these journals (which may only be published in an electronic format) and such access will be immediate. With high speed printing available within the borrowing library, the required document can be downloaded[5] and reproduced upon demand.

The technology of telefacsimile is about twenty years old in terms of its library applications, but recent improvements have led to its increased use by libraries of all types and sizes. With fairly inexpensive equipment, libraries can transmit and receive exact copies of printed or graphic materials over voice grade telephone lines. There have been long standing problems such as the lack of compatibility between various facsimile machines, slow transmission speed, and the need to photocopy journal articles prior to transmission. Transmission speed has now been reduced to approximately one minute for a standard size page, but the other problems remain, including the necessity of a telephone line dedicated solely for use with the telefacsimile machine.

Many libraries are now using this technology to replace former teletype machine used for the transmittal of interlibrary loan forms. Any group of libraries could agree to acquire compatible telefacsimile equipment and send articles, interlibrary loan requests, or messages back and forth. For several very small libraries acting as branches within the same organization, this would be an excellent way to avoid duplication of materials in collections while providing almost immediate access to the combined holdings of all branches. Such an approach will have wide implications for the publishing industry as individuals and libraries refrain from subscribing to journals where only a small percentage of the articles are of interest or are, in fact, read. Instead, individuals will pay for individual articles of interest provided through the library by telefacsimile and from full-text electronic databases. At some point, publishers may no longer feel required to offer printed material, and by authorizing the distribution of single articles by electronic means, they will broaden the user base for all materials for which they hold copyright. In this scenario individuals would request articles regardless of which journal they might formerly have been published in.

Appendix

Outline of a Collection Development Policy
for Company XXX

Objective

To provide a framework within which the library collection can be developed in a planned, consistent, and beneficial manner to meet the information needs of all employees of the company.

I. Scope of the collection
   A. Detailed listing of topics and formats to be included

II. Depth of the collection
   A. Collection levels to be coordinated with topics and formats[6]
   1. Comprehensive: Collect all significant works for a defined field. The intent is to be as exhaustive as possible.
   2. Research: Collect all major published source material that would be required for writing dissertations or pursuing independent research. Includes important reference works, abstracting and indexing services, an extensive collection of journals. (Most special libraries collect at this level for selected subject areas).
   3. Study: A collection adequate for limited or generalized purposes, secondary works, and representative journals. May be directed toward either initial or advanced study.
   4. Basic: A very selective collection that introduces a subject, but depends primarily upon sources of information held elsewhere. Includes some basic reference tools and selected important works and a few of the most important journals in the field. (Most special libraries would provide this type of coverage for some related disciplines that support subjects developed at the research level).
   5. Minimal: Collect a few basic works and not much else. (This level would probably be used extensively by most special libraries for disciplines of very limited interest to the organization or institution).

III. Language
   A. English is the predominant language of scientific literature,

ranging from a low of 50.3 percent of material in the field of chemistry to a high of 82.3 percent in engineering. (Based on an analysis of abstracting and indexing services.[7]) Some one-person libraries may have a greater need than others for foreign language material in the collection.

1. Subject coverage within the scope statements should indicate which foreign languages, if any, are to be collected.

IV. Currency

A. Clear guidelines should define the time periods to be included in the collection. Many small libraries collect only recent material because they support business applications. Limited room retained for housing a collection may dictate that only current materials be retained.

V. Weeding

A. Most small libraries will need to limit the size of the collection because of space limitations. The criteria to be used for the planned removal of material should be part of this policy. A frequency schedule for weeding, as well as the procedure for disposing of materials, should also be included.

VI. Budget Allocations

A. Small libraries may allocate their acquisition budgets between subject areas on an informal basis. If there is a need to ensure consistent expenditure percentages by subject area or material format, then the formula or means of allocation should be included in the collection development policy.

VII. Gift policy

A. Gifts may be important because of limited resources. Policies in this area must protect the library so that unwanted material can be disposed of freely.

VIII. Exchange

A. Materials received through exchange agreements can help stretch a small budget. The intent of exchange and methods to be pursued should be included in the policy.

IX. Selection sources

A. Many libraries use basic lists or bibliographies to identify materials to be added to the collection. If these are regularly used, they should be identified in a list that is part of the policy.

X. Policy Review

A. The collection development policy for Company XXX will be reviewed annually by the librarian. Changes will be incorporated and the policy submitted for approval.

1. Approval of the policy might be appropriate for a library committee, or by the person to whom the librarian reports.

Notes

1. Integrated Library System (ILS) is a computerized system providing the library functions of acquisitions, cataloging, serials, circulation, interlibrary loan, administrative reporting, and some aspects of reference. The ILS operates from a master bibliographic file that forms the basis for an Online Public Access Catalog (OPAC). This replacement for the card catalog is searched electronically from terminals within the library and often from remote sites using microcomputers and modems for dial-up access. All library functions are performed with data from the master bibliographic file through online terminals so that updated information is immediately available for all necessary library operations. For example, once a user has selected a book from the OPAC, it is charged out electronically during the circulation function and the OPAC is changed to reflect that the item is charged out, and when it is due to be returned. Some of the more familiar commercial or marketed integrated library systems include OCLC's LS2000, GEAC, CLSI, and Georgetown's LIS. For more information see chapter 10 and the chapter bibliography.

2. NTIS (National Technical Information Service), *Products & Services Catalog* (Springfield, Va.: U.S. Department of Commerce, 1988).

3. Bernan Associate, *Catalog of Standing Order Titles of U.S. Government Publications* (Lanham, Md.: Bernan Associates, 1985).

4. Online vendors are providers of bibliographic databases and/or copies of the fulltext articles represented by the bibliographic citations. In some instances it is possible to conduct an online search and also request needed fulltext documents at the same time. Users have a way of immediately ordering needed documents online.

5. Downloaded means that information available in online databases can be electronically transferred to the user's microcomputer and placed on a diskette or hard disk for further use. By means of downloading, a user is able to complete a search of a database, transfer citations retrieved to the microcomputer environment for search refinement and printing, thereby disconnecting from the host computer network and the related telecommunication charges.

6. D. L. Perkins, ed., *Guidelines for Collection Development* (Chicago: American Library Association, 1979).

7. K. Subramanyam, *Scientific and Technical Information Resources* (New York: Marcel Dekker, 1981).

Suggested Readings

Aluri, R., and J. S. Robinson. *A Guide to U.S. Government Scientific and Technical Resources*. Littleton, Colo.: Libraries Unlimited, 1983.

Bastile, J. D., and C. J. Mankin. "A Simple Objective Method for Determining a Dynamic Journal Collection." *Bulletin of the Medical Library Association* 68 (October 1980): 357–66.

Bell, J. A. et al. "Methodology for the Comparison of Book Jobber Performance." *Bulletin of the Medical Library Association* 70 (April 1982): 229–31.

Boucher, V. *Interlibrary Loan Practices Handbook*. Chicago: American Library Association, 1984.

Brandon, A. N., and D. R. Hill. "Selected List of Books and Journals for the Small Medical Library." *Bulletin of the Medical Library Association* 77 (April 1989): 139–175.

Conway, S., K. Gallagher, and B. Halbrook. "Selection and Acquisitions Manual Development." *Bulletin of the Medical Library Association* 67 (January 1979): 54–58.

Dellman, B. S. "Tailoring Periodical Collections to Meet Institutional Needs." *Bulletin of the Medical Library Association* 72 (April 1984): 162–67.

Evans, E. A. "Microcomputers: An Interlibrary Loan Application." *Special Libraries* 75 (January 1984): 17–27.

Ford, S. *The Acquisition of Library Materials*. Rev. ed. Chicago: American Library Association, 1978.

Grant, M. M., and Riva Berleant-Schiller. *Directory of Business and Financial Services*. 8th ed. New York: Special Libraries Association, 1984.

Grieder, Ted. *Acquisitions: Where, What, and How*. Westport, Conn.: Greenwood Press, 1978.

Hahn, H. *Technical Services in the Small Library*. Chicago: American Library Association, 1987.

Hunt, D. L. "Sources of Patent Copies." *Science & Technology Libraries* 2 (Summer 1982): 69–78.

Kaiser, F. E. *Handling Special Materials in Libraries*. New York: Special Libraries Association, 1974.

Magrill, R. M., and D. J. Hickey. *Acquisitions Management and Collection Development in Libraries*. Chicago: American Library Association, 1984.

Marin, J. A., and S. B. Manch. "Library Weeds." *Bulletin of the Medical Library Association* 59 (October 1971): 599–602.

Newman, W. B. "Acquiring Technical Reports in the Special Library: Another Package for Information Transfer." *Science & Technology Libraries* 2 (Summer 1982): 45–67.

New York Academy of Medicine. *The New York Academy of Medicine Library*

Collection Development Policy. New York: The Academy, 1982.

Pedersen, W. A. "Graphing: A Tool for Collection Development." *Bulletin of the Medical Library Association* 74 (July 1986): 262–64.

Perkins, D. L., ed. *Guidelines for Collection Development*. Chicago: American Library Association, 1979.

Reed, M. H. *The Copyright Primer for Librarians and Educators*. Chicago: American Library Association, 1987.

Resources and Technical Services Division. Collection Development Committee. American Library Association. *Guidelines for Collection Development*. Chicago: American Library Association, 1979.

Roper, F. W., and J. A. Boorkman. *Introduction to Reference Sources in the Health Sciences*. 2d ed. Chicago: Medical Library Association, 1984.

Segal, J. *Evaluating and Weeding Collections in Small and Medium-sized Public Libraries: The CREW Method*. Chicago: American Library Association, 1980.

Subramanyam, K. *Scientific and Technical Information Resources*. New York: Marcel Dekker, 1981.

Tucci, V. K. "Online Ordering of Sci-tech Materials." *Science & Technology Libraries* 2 (Summer 1982): 27–44.

Tucker, J. C., and E. Cerutti. "A Guide to Locating Sources of Foreign Scientific and Technical Publications." *Science & Technology Libraries* 2 (Summer 1982): 79–111.

7 Organizing the Collection

There are a number of considerations concerning the organization of the collection in the very small library which need to be addressed. One of the overriding concerns has to do with the needs of the library's users: How will these users approach the collection in search of information? Answers to this question can be found through conducting a user study (discussed in chapter 1). A second consideration concerns different types and formats of materials. A third consideration involves the selection of a classification scheme. Finally, subject access to library materials must be considered and different approaches to subject access accommodated.

For each type of material held by the library—monographs, serials, technical reports, audiovisuals—two types of access must be provided. The first of these is physical access: how the materials are to be arranged on the shelves, placed in files, housed in cabinets, and so on. The second type of access has to do with the variety of approaches a user might employ to identify materials of interest.

Physical access to materials

Classification

Classification of the monograph collection is particularly important in the very small library. Books need to be placed on the shelves in some logical and convenient fashion so that library users can help themselves as much as possible, for there will be occasions when the librarian must be absent from the library. The reshelving of materials should also be as simple and free of error as possible.

The Dewey Decimal and Library of Congress classification systems are the two major classification systems used in this country. Both of these systems are enumerative, which means that subjects are usually spelled out in detail and reflected by an appropriate number in the system's classification schedule.

If the very small library is a highly specialized one, like a hospital library, some other classification system for its particular field may be available (like the one produced by the National Library of Medicine).

For a monograph collection that covers many areas of knowledge, none of which are highly specialized or extensively developed, the Dewey Decimal system is probably an appropriate choice. A great deal of time can be saved if the subjects in a collection can be readily adapted to the Dewey classification schedules. Use of the Dewey system under these circumstances usually results in short classification numbers (call numbers) that provide ease of use for both the librarian and the library user. For small libraries with rather specialized collections devoted to a few well-defined areas of knowledge, the use of the Dewey system may not be appropriate. Instead, the Library of Congress (LC) classification may be suitable because of its well-developed (enumerated) schedules for the specialized areas represented by the library's collection.

Regardless of which system is chosen, the librarian should use classification numbers that have been previously established by some other source whenever possible. Some of the sources from which the librarian may take these numbers include card sets provided by commercial vendors or the printed LC cards, published book announcements, cataloging in publication data found in most English language monographs on the verso of the title page, or from a bibliographic utility such as Online Computer Library Center, Inc. (OCLC). A fair amount of the librarian's time can be saved if she is willing to accept someone else's classification number.

Original classification systems

In the very small library, greater simplicity may be achieved through the use of some "in-house" classification or shelf arrangement. Placing materials on the shelf in alphabetical order by author is often the simplest way to meet users' needs. However, one of the major advantages of a subject classification scheme such as Dewey or LC is that it brings related materials together in proximity on the shelves and facilitates browsing. This can also be achieved to a limited extent with an alphabetical arrangement by grouping materials by general subject area and then filing individual books by author within each subject grouping.

The disadvantage of any type of classification scheme is that a book containing several different subjects can only be placed in one shelf location. This will probably not present any real problem for the very small library since additional subject features of a work can be brought out through the subject section of the card catalog.

For certain libraries, none of the means of classification discussed up to now will suffice. Users of a particular library may require greater subject access to materials that can only be provided through a synthetic classification system. Such a system allows for enumeration by the librarian at the time classification numbers are assigned. This is in contrast to the predetermined enumeration found in LC and Dewey schedules. If detailed subject analysis of materials is required, then such synthetic systems as the Universal Decimal System should be investigated before deciding on the best system to use. For the needs of the very small library, the simpler the system chosen, the better it will fit the time constraints of the small library operation.

As a final alternative, the librarian may design a unique, individualized classification scheme. This is perfectly acceptable once the librarian has determined that other available systems are not suited to a particular library setting. Original classification systems may require more of the librarian's time because all of the classification work has to be done within the library. It may prove to be more practical to select the best system already available, accept numbers from other sources, and keep the operation as simple as possible.

Classification and shelving of different types of materials

In the very small library, the monograph collection may be the only classified material. It makes a great deal of sense to avoid classification of the journal collection entirely, and to separate this from other types of library materials. Because most small libraries will probably have fewer than one hundred active serials, these can easily be arranged by title. Even collections of several hundred periodicals do not present any real problems if organized alphabetically so that patrons can easily locate titles of interest.

Periodicals are frequently the most heavily used library materials and therefore require a clear indication of where and how they are arranged on the shelves. The more effective the means of conveying this information, the less time the librarian will have to spend in repeated explanations. One must make clear how titles are filed—either word-by-word ignoring prepositions, articles, and other nonsignificant words; or word-by-word employing every title word in filing after initial articles. Extensive use of shelf guides called "dummies," which refer users to correct locations, should cut down on the number of times the librarian has to leave other duties to assist a user in the periodical section.

Other types of library materials may also require or benefit from being housed separately from the monograph collection. Technical report literature is often best filed by report number with subject access provided through the card catalog or by some other search mechanism. This same means of access applies to maps, audiovisual materials, pamphlets, newspapers, and so on. Whenever materials are housed in separate locations, additional signs will probably be required to aid library users. Library signs are an important tool for librarians who have little time to devote to user inquires.

Another technique that is useful in small libraries is to interfile all types of materials in one shelf arrangement. In this way, library users at the shelf can see all materials that the library has on any given subject, regardless of format. The major disadvantage is that different sizes and shapes are not all suited to standard library shelving. This may require more of the librarian's time in shelving and retrieving items from the collection than if materials are segregated by format.

Subject access to library materials

The subject approach chosen for library materials will depend on the information needs of the library's users. If one expects users to find their own materials by browsing at the shelves, then some type of simple subject grouping of materials may be the most appropriate. For example, all monographs on liability insurance could be grouped together. If patrons are likely to browse in a card catalog rather than at the shelves, then some type of general subject grouping in the card catalog will be most useful. Most librarians will find that many users use a combination of these two approaches when seeking information on a given subject. They may first look up the subject in the card catalog to locate the correct classified portion of the collection, and then go to that section and browse.

Small libraries that serve a clientele with very specialized needs often must provide a rather sophisticated means of subject access. One way to determine the degree of subject access required is to evaluate user searches as being either single access or coordinate (multiple access) searches.

Single access searches are performed when the subject of the search can be expressed with one or more terms that fully describe the information required. For example, a user may require information on measles or German measles. This type of search requires that the librarian or user consult the catalog (or whatever search file is used to record library materials) under the access points of measles or German measles. A coordinate search on this same topic, for example, might involve information on the treatment of measles in the elderly. In this case there are three access points—treatment, measles, and the elderly—and all three of these must be included (coordinated) in any material retrieved. Some information requests might involve a coordinate search for a large number of different subjects, for example, a search on the occurrence of German measles in elderly patients who are also undergoing drug therapy for chronic heart conditions. This search actually involves the coordination of four separate subjects—German measles, the elderly, drug therapy, and chronic heart disease.

Effective coordinate searches are almost impossible to perform manually, and the card catalog in most libraries is not very useful for anything but single access searches. Traditionally, most libraries have not assigned more than three subject headings to any one monograph and, consequently, the exhaustive subject detail in many works is not brought out in the card catalog. This will undoubtedly change as more and more libraries install online public access catalogs and seek to improve the usefulness of the monograph collection through greater subject analysis. This will be particularly important for the small library with a limited collection.

Subject heading lists

One of the secrets to providing subject access for users while conserving the time of the librarian is to use an existing subject heading list that can serve as the basis for organizing the library's collection. Two of the best known general lists in use are the LC and Sears lists. These may not be very suitable for the small specialized library, but other more suitable lists may exist. For example, *Medical Subject Headings* (MESH) is now a standard in medical libraries. Such lists can be modified as local needs dictate, but they do provide a ready-made subject authority and ensure that materials are analyzed and described in a consistent manner as they are added to the collection. If a subject heading list is available it eliminates the need to create a subject authority file on three-by-five cards. Headings in the list can be checked off as they are used, and modifications or additions of new subject headings can be placed in appropriate locations within the printed list. A copy of the subject heading list should be available to library users to assist them in their own subject searches.

It may be that a particular subject heading list can provide for some coordination of subject concepts. For example, "German measles" is a subject heading that one would expect to find in a specialized subject heading list. However, one might also find that the creators of the list have provided a coordinated heading for chronic heart disease as well as other compound subject approaches. This type of so-called precoordination means that some coordination is provided at the time materials are processed into the library's collection rather than at the time a subject search is performed. For example, a subject card for the catalog might have the already coordinated heading, "Chronic heart disease," and the user would find this specific aspect of heart disease as part of a single access subject search.

The librarian might also wish to consider the use of precoordination in attempting to modify or add new headings to an existing subject heading list. The primary consideration should be to provide subject access points that will be highly relevant to the majority of information requests of the library's users.

In addition to the traditional catalog, there are a number of manual information retrieval search files which might be useful when organizing specialized materials such as internal reports, photograph collections, reprints, patents, and similar kinds of materials. Many of these involve constructing a specialized thesaurus to be used for a specific field. In the past, some of these systems have attempted to provide a manual means of performing coordinate searches. Now that microcomputers and online access to databases are so widespread, most of these manual systems have been replaced with more effective electronic search mechanisms.

Complex subject searches

When subject searches depend upon the coordination of two or more concepts, it becomes increasingly difficult for the librarian to identify materials that contain the needed information. The advent of online computer searching of bibliographic files has greatly increased the librarian's ability to perform accurate and highly efficient coordinate searches. Online bibliographic searching may be the single most effective means of conserving the librarian's time while providing a high level of personalized service to the library's users. A number of online database vendors are currently economically available to even the smallest of libraries.

There is considerable debate as to whether or not the person seeking information should be present when the librarian performs an online search or if, with the advent of user-friendly search systems, the user should conduct his or her own searches. Regarding the first issue, it may be more effective if the user is present when the search is conducted; however, many librarians feel that with a thorough presearch interview, there is no reason why the requester has to be present for the actual search. It is likely that the user's presence will extend the time required by the search because of the interaction that takes place with the user present. The librarian and user should decide together whether it would be important for the user to browse or have the advantage of serendipity during an online search. The second issue brings about the question of whether or not patrons would prefer to conduct their own searches. User-friendly systems should probably be available to those who do wish to conduct their own searches. Some users, however, will never want to do their own searching no matter how friendly or easy to use the system is. In any event, the librarian must make sure that users are fully informed about limitations to systems and approaches being used, and that they are aware of additional sources of information that might also be considered.

Single access searches

Most of the subject access provided through the card catalog is by means of single access searches. The use of cards in drawers does not lend itself to coordination at the time of searching. Online catalogs have the capability of overcoming these limitations if monographs receive full subject analysis. There are several things a librarian can do, however, to facilitate the use of the library's card catalog and still save time.

One way to conserve the librarian's time in the maintenance of the card catalog is to separate the subject portion of the catalog from the author and title portions. This separation may even facilitate subject searching in the catalog, but most library users seem to fair about the same whether the catalog is in dictionary arrangement or in a divided format. Another time-saving consideration involves the extensive use of guide cards in the catalog to indicate the presence of material on a particular subject. This eliminates the need to type the subject heading on each card, and when the subject headings need to be changed, as they often do, it is a simple matter to replace only the one subject guide card. No guide cards would be made for subjects until the library actually acquires material on that particular subject.

The use of cross references is another device that is necessary to provide consistency in accessing subjects. Cross references allow catalog users to identify the correct subject headings to search. The two principal forms used are the "see . . ." reference, which directs users from synonyms and other terms they might think of to terms that are part of the subject heading structure used in the catalog, and the "see also . . ." reference, which directs catalog users to additional sources of information on related topics.

Highlighting of catalog entries

The use of highlighting in the card catalog is another means of conserving the librarian's time. In order to eliminate the need to add subject headings and new entries to individual cards, a marking pen can be used to highlight the filing entries on individual cards.[1] The librarian can mark through the filing entry so that one card is filed under the main entry which is indicated by highlighting that portion of that card. Another card is filed under a subject heading as highlighted at the bottom of the card. Other cards would be highlighted for other subject headings and added entries until all the entries that the librarian wished to use had been highlighted individually. This is, of course, facilitated by the librarian's willingness to accept cataloging copy prepared by others. The librarian may also add his or her own subject headings and supplemental entries as local needs dictate. This method is particularly helpful to the librarian if he has someone else to file the cards in the catalog.

If the monograph collection is the principal source of information for a library's users, some of the shortcuts mentioned above may actually be a disservice to the librarian and users of the library. It may be more important to analyze monographs in depth and to assign multiple subject headings so that a greater variety of access points are provided through the card catalog. Periodical articles are frequently indexed to a depth of twelve or more subject headings by some indexing services, and it may be that the importance of monographs in some small libraries warrants a similar depth of analysis. This would require a great expenditure of the librarian's time at the stage when materials are analyzed and added to the collection, but at least an equal amount of time would be saved at the search stage, and the quality of service provided by the library would be considerably enhanced.

This chapter has concentrated on the process of adding monographs to the catalog, but all types of materials should be represented through the author, title, and subject portions of the catalog. Even if journals are not classified, they should still be identified in the card catalog with title and subject(s) cards. Materials such as technical reports might be classified and filed in the monograph collection, or they can be shelved separately. In either case, they should be available to anyone looking in the card catalog. The same holds true for audiovisual materials. In any approach to organizing materials for the small library, the librarian must always consider the needs of the users and select the technique that is least time-consuming but still effective.

Note

1. Filing entries consist of the main entry, subject headings, and added entries. These are found in several fixed locations on catalog cards. The following example of a catalog card may help illustrate the filing entries to be highlighted for filing purposes:

> Smith, James John, 1914-
>   Circulatory physiology, the essentials /
> James J. Smith, John P. Kampine.—Baltimore /
> Williams & Wilkins, c1979.
>   xix, 322 p. : ill. ; 24 cm.
>   Includes index
>
>
>   1. Blood circulation   I. Kampine, John P.
>   II. Title

James John Smith is the main entry for this work and one card in the set would be highlighted by marking through his name and filing that card in the card catalog under "Smith." Only one subject heading "Blood circulation" is identified for this work. Subject headings appear at the bottom of the card and are identified by arabic numbers. The added entries are designated by roman numerals and there are two such added entries for this work. Both the second author "Kampine" and the title could be used as filing entries in the card catalog and these would be highlighted on the appropriate card serving as that particular filing entry. This monograph would require four cards if the main entry and all of the subject and added entries were to be used as filing locations in the card catalog.

Suggested Readings

American Library Association. *American Library Association Filing Rules*. Chicago: American Library Association, 1980.

Corbin, B. G. "Effective Use of OCLC in a One-person Astronomy Library." *Special Libraries* 73 (April 1982): 151–54.

Darling, Louise, ed. *Handbook of Medical Library Practice*. 4th ed. Vol. 1, *Public Services in Health Sciences Libraries*. Chicago: Medical Library Association, 1982.

———. *Handbook of Medical Library Practice*. 4th ed. Vol. 2, *Technical Services in Health Sciences Libraries*. Chicago: Medical Library Association, 1983.

Gorman, Michael. *The Concise AACR2*. Chicago: American Library Association, 1981.

Gorman, Michael, and P. W. Winkler, eds. *Anglo-American Cataloging Rules*. 2d ed. Chicago: American Library Association, 1978 and revisions.

Herdman, M. M., and Jeanne Osborn. *Classification: An Introductory Manual*. 3d ed. Chicago: American Library Association, 1978.

Hoduski, Bernadine, ed. *Cataloging Government Documents: A Manual of Interpretation for AACR2*. Chicago: American Library Association, 1984.

Luthin, Patricia. "Cataloging Marketplace." *Library Hi Tech* 1 (Fall 1983): 55–62.

Uhlan, Miriam, ed. *Guide to Special Issues and Indexes of Periodicals*. 3d ed. New York: Special Libraries Association, 1985.

Weihs, Jean, Shirley Lewis, and Janet Macdonald. *Nonbook Materials: The Organization of Integrated Collections*. 2d ed. Chicago: American Library Association, 1980.

8 Meeting Information Needs
Direct Services

It is in the area of direct user services that the complete purpose for the library's existence, the combined efforts of all individuals involved in library matters, and the effectiveness of the very small library all come together. Provision of information is the end goal for most small libraries and certainly for most special libraries. Since the term "information" can be interpreted very broadly (including education, recreation, etc.) this goal is tenable for all types of small libraries.

If the very small library is organized and operated in the most efficient and effective manner possible, a large amount of the librarian's time can be spent providing direct user services. Every librarian should work toward this, for it may be the deciding factor in whether the library is to grow and prosper or cease to exist.

Not all small libraries will want or need to offer all of the same direct user services. A user study should indicate the desirability and importance of a variety of the different service approaches discussed in this chapter. These include ready reference service, bibliographic searching, indexing, abstracting, translating, editorial assistance, selective dissemination of information, instruction in library use, consultation on information system design, and the circulation of materials.

Ready reference

Ready reference is the foundation upon which all services are built in almost any library. It involves seeking answers to factual questions. The time involved in the search is usually short, although for some ready reference questions, no answers are ever found. In the latter case, the librarian may spend extensive amounts of time in the search and eventually carry the question to the grave, still seeking that elusive answer.

A user study conducted by Voigt identified three recurring information needs of most scientists, and these are probably encountered by most individuals in connection with their work. The first of these is for *current awareness*—the need to be aware of what others in a particular field are doing. This includes the need to be aware of what is happening in related disciplines even though the individual's work is not directly related to those disciplines. The second need is for *everyday information*. This must be satisfied in order for the current research or work in progress to proceed. Finally, there is the retrospective or *exhaustive* need. This is the need to gain a thorough knowledge or overview of everything that has been published on a given topic.

The ready reference function of the library attempts to provide answers to everyday questions. Sample ready reference questions include: What is the melting point for this substance? Where can I write to obtain this information? What is the definition of the term listed here? Where can I find a short, authoritative description of this method of testing? To address the above questions, libraries typically acquire a number of directories, dictionaries, encyclopedias, and handbooks, and arrange these in a ready reference section that is near both the telephone and user service points.

Currently, more and more libraries are utilizing automated approaches to ready reference service in addition to traditional reference collections. As more ready reference books become available online and in electronic formats, the physical presence of the ready reference collection in the library is likely to diminish. Another means of speeding the reference process for some libraries has been to build files of recurring ready reference questions. It can be anticipated that microcomputers will be used to store such files, and that the time spent in locating many ready reference answers will be greatly reduced. The same computer terminals can be used to access online databases. Bibliographic and full-text databases can be used not only for their overall relevance, but also to draw out specific facts for ready reference functions. For example, libraries can now have access to some journals in an electronic format. There may be specific facts contained in the articles in these journals that would answer specific ready reference questions and the microcomputer will be used increasingly for such purposes.

The librarian in the very small library should be highly informed about the ready reference capabilities of any of the works in the library and very familiar with the content of the materials in the ready reference collection. Outside sources, such as other librarians and online databases, are also important in bringing speedy access to information. Fast response time may be critical in the small library, where one has to move on quickly to the next request. In addition, the ability of the very small library to respond to ready reference questions effectively will play a major role in the public image of the library.

One of the greatest criticisms of ready reference service in libraries has been of the reliance on printed sources for answers. This often means that the answer supplied to a given question is no longer current. For example, an executive wishing to write to the president of an organization must have the name and address of the current president. Printed directories, even those of very recent publication date, may not reflect the fact that the presidency has recently changed. The librarian must aid in evaluating the validity of the information retrieved. In this example, the correspondence would probably eventually reach the correct president, but it is up to the librarian to decide if a more recent source of information is needed. Depending upon the nature of the request, it may be that a telephone call to the headquarters of this organization is needed to ensure the accuracy of the information provided to the user.

Bibliographic searching

Bibliographic searching is currently in a stage of transition. The technique of the manual search is rapidly being replaced by online searching of databases. Manual searching was required before 1970 because there were no appropriate online database systems available; today, any one librarian would have difficulty keeping track of the several hundred databases that are available through the major online database vendors. More and more such databases are becoming available for use within libraries without the need for telecommunication links because of compact disc technology. Manual literature searching may still be employed today when the search requires a single access point, that is, for the works of an author, or works on a single subject. However, even in these cases, it is doubtful whether the manual method is preferable to an online approach if the latter is available. An online search may save large amounts of time just by the fact that citations are printed out rather than hand copied by the librarian as in the case of a manual search.

The librarian in the small library must be concerned with finding needed information as quickly as possible, and familiarity with an online system and the relevant databases probably makes the online alternative most desirable in virtually all cases. The chief advantage and strength of online searching, in addition to the speed at which pages can be electronically turned and citations printed, is the ability of the searcher to coordinate, combine, and modify numerous subject headings in a single search. This greatly increases both the specificity of the search and the probability that articles retrieved will be on the desired subject. With full-text databases, in which entire articles are online for searching instead of just document surrogates (consisting of index terms, titles, and/or abstracts), it is increasingly possible to retrieve highly relevant documents.

Bibliographic searching is frequently linked to the need for exhaustive or retrospective information that occurs when one is preparing a research proposal or has completed some research and is writing a report or paper. Bibliographic searching may also be required when an individual wishes to obtain current information on a particular topic. For example, a physician faced with a patient's condition that he has not encountered previously would need a few good articles on that condition; an engineer moving to a new application for a substance might like recent articles describing other applications for the same material.

Bibliographic searching may also be part of the process of answering everyday information needs. Much of the information that eventually ends up in handbooks (compilations of standardized data) is first published in isolated journal articles. These specific facts are needed to meet everyday information needs and may be uncovered through the bibliographic search process. As more full-text systems become available, the use of bibliographic searching for this purpose will become more widespread.

One of the controversies about bibliographic searching is in the evaluation of the outcome of the search procedure. Even librarians without subject expertise should be able to go through a list of citations retrieved in a search and eliminate those that are clearly not relevant to the search request. Once the initial selection is made, then the user should turn to the document surrogates (elements in the bibliographic citations) to identify references for which he wishes to receive the entire document. A major problem in this review process is that the individual's search request represents only a fraction of the user's information interests and needs. The search result is a response to a specific information need at a given point in time, but it is only part of a wider and more comprehensive series of associated information needs. The librarian looks at the search retrieval in light of the specific information request. The user evaluates the search retrieval in light of his or her total information needs. As a consequence, the two individuals frequently differ as to whether or not a particular document is relevant.

The end product of the bibliographic search, whether manual or online, is the provision of relevant documents. Many librarians have been overly concerned with access to document surrogates without a similar emphasis on acquiring the complete article. Because the provision of articles can be costly and time consuming, the very small library should instruct the user to request complete articles from the search bibliography only for very relevant citations. Once these are selected, the library should be able to respond quickly by providing photocopies and using interlibrary loan when necessary.

One approach that is being employed by some libraries is to download bibliographic retrieval for a search on a microcomputer and then refine the search so that the user only receives a bibliography of citations for which the library has journal holdings. This means that articles should be immediately available provided that the library does not circulate its journal collection. This is an acceptable approach as long as the user is aware that only a portion of the relevant literature is actually being presented in response to the search request.

Bibliographic searching can have a great impact upon the library's interlibrary loan operation. Depending upon the databases being searched, the library may have much of what is needed or may have virtually none of the titles retrieved. Because of the need to comply with copyright laws and guidelines, librarians will more and more come to depend upon ordering documents from worldwide vendors whose business is the provision of copies of journal articles. It seems likely that in the future some libraries that provide large numbers of photocopies to other libraries will elect to get out of this business by contracting with a private vendor who would then use the library's collection to provide the needed documents. In this way, the library would eliminate the need to staff and finance an in-house document delivery operation, which is a tremendous drain upon library resources. At the same time, the library whose collection fulfills the document request would also be compensated by the private vendor by sharing in profits received from the documents delivered. Such arrangements will eliminate what now appears to be "free" document delivery, but has in reality often been a financial burden on the "lending" library.

For the very small library, the ability to order a needed document immediately at the time an online search is conducted, with next-day delivery in many instances, will eliminate the need to house infrequently used journals. When full-text systems become widely available online, the small library will be able to download needed textual portions and use a high-speed printer to make documents available instantly. There are some telefacsimile/microcomputer interfaces that make this type of operation possible today. Of course, copyright laws and guidelines must be observed with any document delivery service. In the not too distant future, the need for interlibrary loan systems as we know them today may well be largely limited to rarely held materials that libraries are willing to make available to users in other libraries, and other older materials not available in machine readable form.

Indexing

Indexing is the process of identifying important concepts, subject headings, or "identifiers" for a particular document or article, and using these to provide a means for retrieving needed documents through some search mechanism. Indexing is a time-consuming process involving considerable amounts of planning and a thorough awareness of the needs of the library's users. Probably the only time that the librarian in a small library should consider providing any indexing is when the library acquires a needed body of documents that are, or would be, heavily used if they were adequately indexed.

Some small libraries may have internal technical report collections. Such materials, often produced by the parent organization (perhaps requiring restricted access) could be indexed for greater utilization. A variety of indexing systems can be chosen for this purpose. These range from noncontrolled vocabulary approaches based on title indexing to controlled vocabulary approaches with the construction of a highly detailed thesaurus. In the former, each significant word in the title would serve as an index entry. In the latter, a thesaurus of accepted index entries would control for synonyms. A number of useful publications on these topics are included in the reading list for this chapter. There are pros and cons to the different systems. The needs of the library's users should be foremost when deciding which system to employ. Systems that do not provide vocabulary control will require less time from the librarian, but they may not be helpful to users. There are several software packages now available for microcomputers that would enable the librarian to devise an automated indexing system for a specialized document collection. This may be the preferred alternative because of the time that can be saved during both the indexing and retrieval stages.

Occasionally there may be a need to index a particular journal that is of interest to the library's users but which is not indexed by any of the printed or online indexing services. Such indexing need not take up too much time if a simple indexing system is selected. The construction of a thesaurus of fairly broad subject headings limited to some two to three hundred concepts might serve for this purpose.

With microcomputers available for such applications, even the very small library should be able to produce an online database that contains indexing provided by the librarian without extensive effort. Innovations such as microcomputer technology should be taken into consideration when designing any indexing system.

Abstracting

Abstracting is the process of condensing a document into summary form. The summary, depending upon the type of abstract prepared, may or may not serve as a substitute for the original article. Informative abstracts are those intended to provide all the information that the reader of the abstract will need, and thus are often written to serve as substitutes for the original document. Indicative abstracts merely attempt to give the reader some idea of the original document and provide enough information so that the reader can determine whether or not the original document should be consulted.

Abstract writing is usually labor intensive, and few small libraries will want or need to offer such service. However, in the library serving a small engineering or geological firm for example, the librarian may be serving the information needs of as few as half a dozen engineers or geologists. Under such circumstances, the librarian might regularly scan incoming materials and select those pertinent to the research of the library's users. If these materials do not have abstracts, the librarian may produce such abstracts to send to individuals on a research team.

Abstracts might also be written for technical report literature. In general, an abstract conveys more information than an index, and provides a better basis for determining the relevance of an article. Even so, any abstracting system will also need to provide index approaches to enable the abstracts to be retrieved for specific requests. Fortunately, most disciplines are covered by extensive commercial and other nonprofit indexing and abstracting services, and these may be sufficient for the needs of the small library. One should not try to duplicate the work of existing services.

Translating

Approximately 50 percent or more of the world's scientific literature is produced in English. However, this varies greatly depending upon the discipline and the topic being considered. In some fields, such as physics, foreign language literature will occasionally be important to certain library users. The librarian should be aware of this in collection development, and he should provide services that enable library users to secure translations when they are needed. Chances are that most librarians in small libraries will not be familiar with more than one or possibly two foreign languages. A requirement that the librarian be prepared to do translating is probably not appropriate in most cases. Most material in need of translation will usually require both a language facility and some subject knowledge of the material to be translated. In the small library, a translation service would probably make poor use of the librarian's time unless the translation were brief and informal. However, the librarian can facilitate the translation process by being thoroughly familiar with sources for obtaining translations. There are a number of ways in which the small library can obtain translated materials.

One approach to translation service is for the library to subscribe to the literature that provides bibliographic control for translated materials, such as the *Translations Register Index*, produced by the National Translation Center and the *World Transindex*, produced by the World Translation Center. Translations are also found in a number of abstracting and indexing services, including *Government Reports Announcement & Index*. The librarian of the very small library should be familiar with these publications and any other sources available to control access to translated material in disciplines and subjects of interest. The availability of existing translations is important because acquiring copies of such translations is usually relatively inexpensive compared to the cost of having material translated on a contract basis.

Another approach to translation in the small library is to provide a list of translators available to the library's clientele. Such a list can be compiled in a variety of ways. One of the best ways may be to advertise in company or organization publications, or at local universities or multinational organizations in the area. The library should list individuals by language capabilities and subject areas, and then keep the file current. Users in need of translations can have direct access to the file and make their own arrangements for translations and payment. In this way the library provides a needed service but does not get involved in matters of scheduling, payment, etc. Also, since the librarian will usually have no way of evaluating the translation, it is best that the user deal directly with the person doing the translating.

Commercial translation services are available from a number of sources. Brochures describing such services frequently come to the library and these should be retained in a folder for later reference. Such services also advertise in many of the library journals, and these should be noted. Prices vary considerably from service to service, so recommendations from those who have used the services could be very helpful to the librarian. If the library contracts for a translation, the librarian may wish to make a copy of the translation for the library's file before passing it on to the user. Because requests for translations come from users, it will be difficult, in most cases, for the librarian to identify in advance items for which translations should be sought.

Editorial assistance

Editorial assistance is a service designed to aid the library user with the completion of a manuscript prior to submitting it for publication. As with indexing and abstracting, this service is secondary to the primary services of ready reference and bibliographic searching. However, the librarian is ideally suited to assist in certain phases of manuscript preparation. The verification of references can be performed by the librarian in an effective manner through the use of online databases. A few minutes at the terminal may substitute for several hours of page turning by librarians or library users. Some librarians assume additional editorial projects such as proofreading and helping to organize material. However, this is probably not a good idea since the librarian of the very small library has little time and so many other primary functions to perform.

Selective dissemination of information (SDI)

This personalized current awareness service involves formulating a profile that represents the information needs of an individual user or group of users. For example, a chemist might be interested in specific chemical substances; this would form one part of her interest profile. She might also be interested in any work that cites specific authors. The names of these authors would also become part of the SDI profile. Periodically, materials identified as matching profile elements would be brought to the user's attention. This notification could provide either the documents themselves or surrogates (citations and/or abstracts) for the documents.

User profiles should be written down and updated regularly to include changes in an individual's information needs and interests. However, the librarian in the very small library will also need to be aware of these profiles in a general way so that new monographs, reports, journal articles, and other materials acquired can be brought to the attention of those who might be interested. No librarian should try to retain this information mentally. Should a librarian move to a new position, the incoming librarian would have to create an SDI system from the beginning.

Because of the importance of periodical literature in many disciplines, this literature should usually receive the first attention of the librarian. A good practice is to scan the tables of contents of all the journals received by the library each day. This can be done as they are checked in or immediately thereafter. This not only alerts the librarian to what is being published, but it also enables him or her to quickly spot anything that should be called to a user's attention.

As with so many other library services, the use of online databases has had an impact on SDI. Most database vendors provide search systems that offer some type of ranging mechanism by which the librarian is able to limit the search to only select portions of the database. By this means, the librarian can match a user's SDI profile against just the latest or some other relevant portion of the database. By scheduling these searches to coincide with the time that various databases are updated by the vendor, the SDI profile can be matched against only that portion of the database since the last SDI search was conducted. It is also possible for online systems to store SDI profiles, in which case the librarian can recall them when needed. This saves the time of having to enter the profile each time it is to be searched. Some systems not only store such profiles, they also run them automatically for the user on some regular schedule, such as weekly or monthly.

Any such service that offers to save the librarian's time for a reasonable fee should be considered by the librarian of the very small library. The librarian can then make sure that profiles are updated as needed and that documents identified through the SDI search are made available to users.

Any SDI service that covers a wide portion of the literature during the matching process will result in increased pressure on the small library to acquire articles not found in the collection. For example, one of the SDI services offered by a large information service scans articles from some 4,500 journals in the matching process. The result is that the local library is likely to have only a few of the titles that are identified in the SDI match. As previously noted, more and more of these articles will have to be provided through the use of document delivery services from other libraries and document vendors. Future means of acquiring these articles through downloading, telecommunications, videodisk, compact disk, and high-speed printers will dramatically affect both collection development and the ability of the library to provide virtually instant document delivery. Until now, libraries have been largely dependent upon the postal service. In the years ahead, this dependence should all but disappear.

SDI should be part of the operation of the very smallest of libraries, for it provides individuals with information before they are aware of its existence and thus is critical to effective library service. Because SDI service keeps the library before the user's eyes on a regular and continuing basis by constantly providing new information, it is also one of the best means of publicizing the library.

Instruction in library use

An almost opposite approach to the use SDI services is the provision of instruction in library use. Because of a lack of staff in the very small library, there may be a need to provide some type of instruction for potential users in order that they obtain information when the librarian is not there to help or is too busy to do so.

Many special librarians may balk at this suggestion because the credo of the special librarian is to provide service. Special librarians are in place to meet their users' information needs, and librarians are the experts in use of the library and its bibliographic apparatus. Users who attempt to help themselves are often shortchanged because of their lack of expertise in library organization and utilization. In addition, the users may be violating the efficient and effective assignment of duties that is basic to a profit-making organization. Special librarians, especially those in very small libraries, should be experts at finding information, and their library users should be experts at using this information.

Even so, librarians are not "guardians of the temple's secrets," and they should be only too glad to educate others in the mysteries of the library and its role in information transfer. This transfer begins with the creation of information, often resulting from basic research, through its ultimate dissemination, and finally to its re-use, leading to the creation of still more new information. Several approaches to library instruction have been tried, some with more success than others. Library literature is filled with reports of case studies. Many institutions provide general library orientations to reach new employees or students and introduce them to the library. Such orientations usually suffer from trying to provide too much information in too short a time. A quick look at where things are located in the library and some guidelines for use are all that should be involved in a short tour of the library. The most important idea to put across to individuals is that the library can and will help them. Further attempts to instruct users can then focus on individual instruction and formalized bibliographic instruction.

For the librarian who feels a need to educate library users in the bibliographic mechanism of the library, it is best to concentrate on helping users to identify the universe of information resources that are available and those that might be useful to them personally. The actual makeup of each resource and its special features are matters best left to the expert—the librarian. An admirable goal for any library instruction program would be to ensure that those receiving instruction about the library come away thinking that the library is the place to go if they want information. Internalizing this simple linkage between information and the library will do more to further the cause of any organization than all of the formalized bibliographic instruction that might be forced on those who have no inclination to learn such things.

Librarians are continually showing individuals how to find things in the card catalog and how to use indexing and abstracting services. If successful, neither the librarian nor the user really thinks of this as instruction; rather, it is seen as the process of finding needed information. In many settings, however, the user's time should not be spent in this fashion unless there are other benefits to be derived from such an approach.

Consulting on information system design

Consulting on information system design is a rather complicated way of describing a service provided by the librarian outside the library that could be of direct benefit to many individuals within the organization served by the library. Most individuals, whether involved in research, management, or some other phase of operations, have their own personal sources of information that often serve as a principal means of meeting their information needs. These sources are often in the form of reprints, flyers, reports, and documents, housed in vertical files within each person's office. The problem with most of this material is that it is not organized so that retrieval of information is simple and easy. An alphabetical file may enable one to find an article on a particular subject, but it does not facilitate access to particular bits of information contained in articles. For such collections to be fully accessible, some type of indexing system would need to be installed.

Librarians have long been sought as consultants on how office files should be organized for maximum effectiveness. With the advent of the microcomputer and its widespread availability, a useful service for the library to offer would be help in personal information system design. Some of the questions that face the potential user of such a system include: What types of software are needed? What means of retrieval should be provided? How are materials to be stored? What interfaces between files need to be established and maintained? Answering each of these concerns is within the expertise of the librarian who deals with storage and retrieval of information on a daily basis.

It is conceivable that some organizations with electronic storage of personal information files will want to make such files available to everyone within the organization. If information in an individual's files is personally useful, it may be equally useful to others within the organization. Such information sharing will probably not work in a setting where there is competition between individuals. The other side of the argument is that everything in those files is really company property and should be utilized to its fullest for the good of the company.

Consultation in setting up personal information systems should probably not be a highly publicized service of the very small library because there is simply not enough time to devote to such an activity should a number of people request help. However, once a system has been designed for one individual it may be adaptable to other personal files within the organization. As with many other services, the public relations value of providing this kind of consultation service can be very helpful to the small library.

Circulation of materials

There is no separate chapter in this monograph on the circulation of materials because the methods used vary considerably from library to library, regardless of the number of people employed or served by the library. The subject is being treated under direct services because this is the context within which one should design any circulation system. Circulation systems provide management control for the collection, but more importantly, they allow users to utilize information where it is needed. The reason many libraries seem to have such extensive circulation policies is that the circulation function has two conflicting goals. One of these is to enable the individual to have access to information outside the library proper; the other is to make sure that everyone has equal access to library resources. One set of policies strives to place material in users' hands and the other set of policies strives to retrieve these materials so that others may use them. It often appears to the user that he or she is caught in the middle of a system that works but not well.

For most small libraries, the circulation service should be carefully constructed. The public relations value of an effective circulation system is great, but a poor system can have the reverse effect. The system should be as simple as possible while still able to keep track of who has material checked out and when it is due back, as well as any other statistical information the librarian chooses to gather. The small library should have a system that is easy for library patrons to use. The checkout procedure may involve some work, but it should not be a lot of work. If successful, the librarian will not have to stop working in order to check out books. Electronic circulation systems lend themselves to self-operation if designed with bar codes on books and user identification. If one is worried about security for the library collection, a simple electronic system could be developed that would utilize the individual's employment identification card. This card would be "read" along with the identifier for library materials before the electronic security system would allow the user to exit the library without sounding an alarm.

Many librarians seem to suffer from the delusion that it is possible to prevent the occurrence of overdue material by establishing close controls. This includes mailing overdue notices and charging fines for overdue materials. Most small libraries cannot afford to have the librarian spend the time it takes to perform these functions or impose these sanctions. The time of the librarian is too valuable to spend collecting a few pennies in fine money. Most small libraries are within compact or well-defined organizations where it is relatively easy to keep track of the library's clientele. Many small public libraries are not much different in that they are located in small communities and library users are generally known.

Materials will not always be returned on time regardless of the circulation system employed by the library. It will probably save a great deal of time and effort if the librarian waits until an overdue item is needed by someone else. The librarian can then proceed to retrieve the item in the most direct and expeditious fashion— probably by means of a telephone call. In the small public library where the environmental context is much broader, a different system of locating stray materials will probably be needed and employed more frequently. In many organizations, an individual who changes employment must first be cleared by the organization, and this clearance includes the library. However, the public library's users move in and out of the community without any similar means of clearance for library materials.

By keeping the circulation system simple, responsive to individual needs, able to ensure equity of access, and by having the user perform as much of the circulation process as possible, the librarian of the small library should find that the circulation of materials is one of the most heavily used services the library offers and that library users greatly appreciate such a service. Equity of access means simply that there are sufficient library policies to control the length of loan periods while providing more immediate access to materials that are urgently needed. Special librarians, who are themselves cooperative by nature, usually find that library users are willing to return materials when they are needed by others.

Cited Literature

Voigt, M. J. *Scientists' Approaches to Information.* Chicago: American Library Association, 1961.

Suggested Readings

Anders, M. E. "Reference Service in Special Libraries." *Library Trends* 12 (January 1964): 390–404.

Borgman, C. et al. *Effective Online Searching: A Basic Text.* New York: Dekker, 1984.

Chen, Ching-chih, and P. Hernon, eds. *Numeric Databases.* Norwood, N.J.: Ablex Publishing, 1984.

Crum, N. J. "The Librarian-Customer Relationship: Dynamics of Filling Requests for Information." *Special Libraries* 60 (May/June 1969): 269–77.

Fried, A. K., and A. J. Hurlebaus. "A Re-evaluation of Circulation Policies: Overdues Process and Loan Period." *Special Libraries* 72 (July 1981): 284–89.

Hlava, M. *Private File Creation/Database Construction.* New York: Special Library Association, 1984.

Klein, F. "The Translator in the United States." *Science & Technology Libraries* 3 (Winter 1982): 31–46.

Kolner, S. J. "Improving the MEDLARS Search Interview: A Checklist Approach." *Bulletin of the Medical Library Association* 69 (January 1981): 26–33.

Maloney, J. J., ed. *Online Searching Technique and Management.* Chicago: American Library Association, 1983.

Newman, P. E. "The In-house Translator: An Overlooked Specialist." *Science & Technology Libraries* 4 (Fall 1983): 91–97.

Olsgaard, J. K. "Keyword Indexing of a Faculty Reprint Collection." *Bulletin of the Medical Library Association* 69 (October 19, 1981):397–99.

Palmer, R. C. *Online Reference and Information Retrieval.* Littleton, Colo.: Libraries Unlimited, 1983.

Raitt, D., ed. *Introduction to Online Information Systems.* Medford, N.J.: Learned Information, 1984.

White, M. D. "The Dimensions of the Reference Interview." *RQ* 20 (Summer 1981): 373–81.

9 Meeting Information Needs
Indirect Services

Indirect services are those activities that are indispensable in providing users with timely, accurate, and effective information, but do not directly address the specific information needs of users. Many of these functions take place behind the scenes, but it is important that librarians be aware that such functions are not for the convenience or benefit of the library; rather, they facilitate the provision of information to the library user.

Some of the indirect user services that the small library can provide are acquisitions, shelving of library materials, cataloging, new book displays, current awareness services, shelf reading, and record keeping. Each of these is worth some discussion because even though all libraries perform most of these functions, they are often not viewed from the perspective of their impact upon the library user. Some of these topics have been covered in previous chapters, but not from the perspective offered here.

Acquisitions

The selection and subsequent acquisition of material is not done to enhance the size of the library's collection or increase the prestige of the librarian, but to provide information that is needed. Thus, acquisition should emphasize the benefits to users that result from these activities.

The selection function is performed to meet existing and anticipated interests of library users. This means that those doing the selecting have to be highly knowledgeable about what users are currently involved in and what future plans exist for the organization or institution. Only by being intimately involved with the decision making-process of the organization, knowing individuals well, and being aware of areas of research, education, and activity can the librarian anticipate information needs and match these against available materials.

As an indirect user service, the acquisition process concentrates on obtaining needed materials in a timely fashion and, if possible, having them available in the library before they are actually needed. Speed in acquiring materials that have been selected is the key to accomplishing this. It is not unusual in a university library for a faculty member to submit a request for material and find that it has arrived in the library some six months later. Even then, it may not be immediately available to the faculty member until a "rush" processing order has prepared it for circulation. In a special library, particularly a small library, the process must function to the benefit of the user. The need for information is frequently tied to the continued well-being of the organization's research and development. Information must be available at the time it is needed or the research process is slowed and may be negated.

If research needs are anticipated, information may be available in the library before it is actually needed. In some instances, this may influence the research topics undertaken or change the course of existing research. If research topics cannot be fully anticipated, then the need for a particular item usually becomes immediate at some later date and the librarian must skillfully make up for lost time. If future technological applications occur as envisioned, it may become quick and easy to transfer a needed document from one library to another by means of telefacsimile or downloading with high-speed printout. Similar access through CD-ROM (Compact Disk-Read Only Memory) technology also appears imminent. However, until such electronic means are widely available, most small libraries will have to find other ways of expediting the acquisition process.

Advanced payment, telephone orders, direct ordering from the publisher, requesting rush status when orders are placed, or contacting some other library for an urgent interlibrary loan may all be possibilities for the librarian in a small library who is trying to speed up the acquisition process. The librarian may also be able to use his own car to facilitate a quick pick-up of needed material. It should be noted that under rush circumstances, discounts for materials are not usually applicable.

New books display

As new books are received, requests for their purchase should be checked. Books that were ordered at the request of individuals in the organization should be identified, and the user notified that the work has arrived. Should the book be desired immediately, then some form of fast cataloging or processing should be applied so that the work can leave the library until it can be fully processed later on. Books that have not been requested, or that are not needed immediately, should be examined and matched against known user needs and interests within the organization. Books that can be matched to individuals should be brought to their attention. Any new works that are left at this point should be placed in a designated user area to bring them to the attention of all library users. It is usually sufficient to use a few shelves close to the circulation area for this purpose. It is helpful to post a sign indicating that the area is for new arrivals and to maintain some schedule for the placement and removal of books. The librarian may want to distribute on a regular basis a list of new books acquired, perhaps including this information in a library or organizational newsletter.

Books on display can be made available for patron use in different ways. In some libraries, it may be possible to circulate the materials as soon as they have been placed on the display shelves. In this way, users who check the shelves regularly and find items of interest have immediate access to the materials and can take them from the library. Other libraries insist that all materials on display remain there for a set number of days before being allowed to circulate. In this way, everyone has a chance to view them before they disappear into users' hands. Under the second arrangement, it is wise to provide some means of reserving individual books so that when they do become available for circulation, those users who have expressed an interest will have the first opportunity to check them out. If a long waiting list develops, the librarian should consider purchasing duplicate copies of the works in demand.

New book displays require little added effort on the part of the librarian, and they serve as a good means of public relations for the library. Library users are made aware of the materials that the library is acquiring, and many users are pointed to books they might otherwise miss.

A different approach to new book displays might be to display the book jackets instead of the books themselves. Few libraries, other than public libraries, receive or retain many book jackets. Displayed prominently and replaced on a regular basis, these could well serve the same objective as the display of the actual books. Even if new books are allowed to circulate, the book jackets will still alert users to the fact that these books are now part of the library's collection.

Current awareness services

Current awareness services are highly important to most special libraries, and even very small libraries can utilize such services to provide users with information that may be of interest to them without their having to first ask for it. In library parlance there is some confusion between current awareness services and selective dissemination of information (SDI) services. Current awareness service is the more generic term. It includes those services that bring information to the attention of the library's users in a format that requires that each user look through what is provided and decide whether or not it is pertinent to his or her information needs. Any information that is "new" to the recipient of such a service is considered a part of current awareness. SDI services are specifically tailored to meet the information needs of the individual user. The basis for the provision of the SDI service is the user's profile. A more complete discussion of SDI can be found in chapter 8.

There are two basic approaches to the provision of current awareness service in most small libraries. One involves the announcement of journal literature to those who might have a need for it. The other approach involves the production of a library publication that provides the user with a variety of information sources. Although both of these techniques are aimed at a group of users rather than individuals, current awareness services are an important mainstay of special libraries and should be considered as an important indirect user service by the librarian in the very small library.

Journal routing

Informing users of new journal articles is a current awareness service and can be achieved in a number of ways. The routing of select journals to individuals is one way. The librarian can attach a simple name checklist to each journal to be routed. When an individual receives the journal, he scans it for articles of interest, checks off his name, and then passes the journal on to the next name on the routing list. There are a number of disadvantages to this method. One is that the librarian is never sure of the location of any given journal while it is in the routing process. Although this can be overcome by having each user return the journal to the library before it is checked out to the next person on the list, this exacerbates a second disadvantage of such a routing system: information is only current if the individual is not already familiar with that information. If individuals do not complete their use of each journal and expedite its delivery to the next person on the list, the current awareness value of such a system may be limited to only the first one or two names on the routing list. If materials are to be returned to the library each time to be checked out to the next person on the routing list, the delay may obviate the current awareness function.

Another means of journal routing that is probably preferable for most small libraries, is to copy the tables of contents from new journals and send these to the individuals instead of the actual journals. This has the advantage of keeping the journal in the library where it remains accessible to everyone. A variation on this method is to photocopy the tables of contents from several journals, and attach these together and send them out as a table of contents bulletin. Each individual can then look through the tables of contents for journals of interest, and decide which articles to follow up on. Because there is very little time or cost invested by the librarian in this type of current awareness system, multiple copies of the bulletin can be produced to make sure that people receive current listings. An individual requesting the service could receive her own copy of the bulletin, or one copy could serve as many as three or four people by means of the routing slip procedure. The guiding principle should be the ability of the library to maintain the current awareness function of the service.

Another way to route tables of contents is to subscribe to a tables of contents service, such as that provided by the Institute for Scientific Information with its *Current Contents* publication. Because this bulletin appears weekly and is published in a number of different editions that are each devoted to specific disciplines, it is possible to offer a broad disciplinary or interdisciplinary approach to journal literature. A small library might wish to acquire multiple subscriptions (at reduced rates) and provide each individual with a copy, or groups of research personnel could have a copy routed to them weekly. It is important to consider what impact such services may have on the demand for journals that the library does not subscribe to. The librarian should probably anticipate an increase in interlibrary loan requests.

With any of these current awareness approaches, it is important that the librarian monitor the system to ensure that it is working effectively and that changes in the routing pattern occur as individual needs and interests change. It is also important that some means of providing complete journal articles be available for current awareness systems based on journal surrogates. A simple check-off system should be included to enable the user to identify those articles for which copies of the complete articles are needed. Once again, speed in obtaining these articles is necessary if the current awareness function is to be maintained.

Library bulletins

General current awareness within an organization or institution is improved when employees are informed of library materials, ideas, changes, meetings, and other items of information. This can be accomplished by the library through the production of a current awareness bulletin. With this method, each individual is responsible for identifying those items in the bulletin that are of personal interest. The frequency of such a bulletin will depend upon the material that it carries and the needs of the employees of any given organization. In order for it to fulfill a current awareness function, publication on at least a monthly basis will probably be called for.

With the librarian of the small library serving as editor of the bulletin, guidelines should be established to help identify materials to be included in the publication. One possibility is for the librarian to survey the journal, patent, monographic, technical report, and government document literature that arrives in the library and supply citations, and possibly abstracts, for items that need to be brought to the attention of the employees of the organization. Abstracts that are provided in the works themselves can be included, if available. If the abstracts are taken from the publications, then matters of copyright must be considered.

Publication of such a bulletin is time consuming, but it may provide a highly useful current awareness service that is tailored to the needs of a particular organization. There are no limitations on what may appear in the bulletin as long as it is directed toward the current awareness function. The public relations benefits to the library from such a service are excellent.

One possibility for a current awareness bulletin might be the inclusion of a "hot topics" or "current references" section in which the librarian highlights key research issues or problem areas of interest to the organization. A literature search might turn up a number of references from all types of materials. The librarian can then select a few "best" references for abstracting and publication in the bulletin. It is likely that such a literature review will require some subject expertise on the part of the librarian. In any event, it must be clearly stated that the references presented represent only a portion of the total subject literature and that the library will supply comprehensive literature searches upon request.

Shelf reading

Shelf reading is the act of checking the classification numbers assigned to individual books on each shelf to see if they are in the correct sequence and to rearrange them if they are out of order. It is generally considered a thankless job by those who have to perform it. However, it is really a very important indirect user service because any item that is misshelved is, in essence, lost. From the standpoint of the library's users, whenever one is able to go to the shelves and find a book in its correct place, the library has provided an indirect, but highly important user service.

It will be hard for the librarian in the very small library to supply sufficient staff time for a thorough shelf reading schedule, but a regular schedule is important to ensure that the entire collection is checked with the frequency needed. In the absence of other employees, the librarian must take the time to perform this very important, but rather boring function.

Another means of ensuring the integrity of the shelving arrangement for the small library should also be considered: signs encouraging users to place materials they have used in a central location or to leave them on tables will allow the librarian to reshelve virtually all materials used within the library. Ideally, this will mean that the shelves contain fewer misplaced books than if users were to reshelve their own materials. Even so, individuals browsing at the shelves will still remove books and replace them incorrectly on occasion. For small public libraries, books reshelved by users usually present an even greater problem because of the wide diversity among the library users.

Another approach is to devise a shelving system that is so easy and simple that anyone can return books to their proper sequence. It would appear, however, that such a foolproof system has not yet been devised and that shelf reading will remain a necessary function for all libraries.

Library records benefiting the user

Most libraries, even very small ones, generate a number of record-keeping systems. However, records should only be kept if there is a clear need for having such records and they are maintained for some useful and meaningful purpose.

Many of the records that are kept in some libraries appear to be purely for the benefit of the librarian. They are part of library management and mostly are not available in public access areas; however, many of these records are actually generated for the benefit of library users. When viewed from a user perspective, the provision of up-to-date, accurate records can be considered an indirect user service designed to meet individual information needs.

The principal record system that library users need and often depend upon is the catalog of library holdings, which includes the serials holding records. The catalog, whether in traditional card format or in the increasingly popular electronic online format, is the main avenue by which many users approach the library's collection. Generations of library users have received some type of instruction in the makeup and use of the card catalog and they carry such experiences and expectations with them to the very small library. By keeping a consistent and current record of the library's holdings arranged by author, title, and subject, the library provides users with the key to virtually everything the library owns.

The serials records are at least as important as the catalog in most special libraries where journal literature is of primary concern. The serials records of any library should also contain accurate, up-to-date information on each journal that the library has acquired, either on a current or retrospective basis. Information on whether or not volumes are complete is also essential. The serials records should be exceptionally clear so that users can easily interpret the information without assistance from the librarian. If serials are not shelved separately from the book collection in alphabetical order, then shelf locations for the serials should also be identified for the users. For example, if call numbers are used for serials, they should be provided in the serials records so that users do not have to first consult the serials records and then the card catalog to obtain a call number.

Some very small libraries have such severe space limitations that it is difficult if not impossible to allow users to serve themselves. In such settings librarians may retrieve all materials for their users. Such a library could function much like a pharmacy or some other retail outlet where users submit requests at a window or desk and materials are then retrieved by the librarian and returned to the user at the window or desk. Under those conditions library records may not be directly accessible to library users.

Librarians in very small libraries may need to keep other specialized records because they assist the library's users and save the librarian's time. The secret is to make the library as useful for self-service as possible, while ensuring that the librarian is always brought into the picture when needed.

Suggested Reading

LaHood, C. G., and R. D. Sullivan. *Reprographic Services in Libraries: Organization and Administration.* Chicago: American Library Association, 1975.

10 Automation in the Library

Automation in libraries has traditionally meant the use of machines to perform library functions. Early on, typewriters produced cards for the card catalog, microfilm cameras and readers stored information, and turnstiles recorded the number of library users. In more recent times, library automation has come to mean the use of electronic devices that aid in the provision of library services. Specifically, these are computers, although another very popular application has been the employment of electronic security systems.

The history of library automation

Data processing equipment (punch-card equipment) was used in libraries from about 1925 on, but with little enthusiasm or widespread adoption. The first mass-produced computers appeared in the 1950s, and librarians began envisioning their use for a variety of library operations. Because of the need for shared use of large computers and delays in processing time, the immediate access needed for up-to-date library information was not available. Clearly, the use of the costly computer for direct application by small libraries was not practical. Even so, some relatively small special libraries did start producing book catalogs and other automated library files in the 1960s. Some publishers were also beginning to produce their products with the aid of the computer, and the National Library of Medicine began offering a literature search service that involved several days delay between the time the search was submitted and the results were mailed to the user. However, it was not until the advent of online computer systems in the early 1970s that library automation involving the computer really took hold. Since that time the use and number of applications of automation in the library have increased dramatically through the availability of online databases, CD-ROM databases, integrated library systems, microcomputer applications software, and computer assisted instruction. The use of artificial intelligence and expert systems is just now beginning to make its presence felt in the library world.

Online databases

There are now literally hundreds of online databases available to libraries of all sizes through major vendors in the United States. These vendors include both public and private enterprises of which BRS (Bibliographic Retrieval Services), Dialog Information Service, Orbit Search Service, Wilsonline, and the National Library of Medicine are notable examples. Mergers, buyouts, and name changes are becoming a familiar part of this fluid industry.

Databases of interest to libraries have traditionally been bibliographic. However, nonbibliographic databases have become increasingly important and will probably continue to increase in importance for some types of small libraries. For example, the small business or corporate library may have a greater need for facts and figures contained in online databases of company annual reports than for citations and abstracts of articles about some aspect of business or corporate finance. In medicine, an individual might prefer to know the toxic risks of a given chemical rather than be referred to an article in the journal literature that may or may not contain the needed information.

For the small library with limited space, all that is needed in lieu of a subscription to printed abstracts or indexes is a "dumb terminal" (searching and printing capabilities only) plus a modem and telephone line, or a "smart terminal" (microcomputer) plus a modem and telephone line to access online databases. Remote online databases are accessed by arranging with the provider of a database to supply the library with an identification number. The librarian then uses the terminal to call the network that provides the desired database, log into the system, type in the library's identification number for billing purposes, and conduct a search of appropriate databases. Relevant information is then printed out at the library terminal. Subsequently, the library is billed in accordance with its contractual agreement with the database provider. Such charges may consist of a flat rate per hour of use, an algorithm based on selected use parameters, or some other formula agreed upon in the initial contract. This method of searching can eliminate the need to house volumes of printed abstracts and indexes. For example, files of *Chemical Abstracts*, *Biological Abstracts*, and similar services take up many sections of shelving. The small library may be better off obtaining these services electronically and only pay for actual use of the database. As the price of subsidizing printed indexes becomes excessive in the years ahead, it is likely that only online access will be provided by publishers for some of these services.

The principal gain for library users when online database access is provided is the speed and effectiveness of retrieval that is possible. Large files of citations and abstracts that cover many years can be searched in a matter of seconds because of the great speed of computer operation. Complex subject searches consisting of an almost unlimited number of topics can also be executed with an online search system. Such a search in printed indexes would be virtually impossible. For any online searcher, particularly the individual needing information, the chance to experiment, try ideas, and interact with feedback from the search process without any delay enables greater search refinement and a far better match between retrieval and information need than is usually possible with printed sources.

One problem for the librarian of the very small library is the amount of training that is needed in order to become familiar with the search systems that provide databases needed by the library's clientele. Different users will need databases offered by different vendors, and each search system requires some training if the librarian is to become an effective searcher on that particular system. Training sessions are usually offered in a number of locations throughout the country each year and there is usually a charge for such training. It may be difficult for the librarian to get away long enough to take advantage of the training that is offered. Programs offered through local library consortia or other library organizations may be a suitable alternative. Information networks such as

ILLINET or SOLINET (discussed in chapter 14) may also be sources for local training sessions.

Larger libraries are able to assign vendor and database responsibilities among several staff members depending on their knowledge of specific disciplines and familiarity or training in certain systems. The librarian in the small library will have to cover all of the needed vendors and databases with little help unless some type of sharing with other librarians can be worked out. This may result in the librarian's knowing frequently used databases quite well. Others that are used less frequently will require some degree of relearning when they are needed. However, it is important that the librarian be aware of all relevant sources and be able to use those that are most helpful even if their infrequent use makes access slower and more difficult.

More and more librarians are branching out into private business as information brokers and the librarian in the small library will be able to tap these sources when searching expertise is needed. The cost of using unfamiliar databases by this method may be far less than having an untrained or inexperienced librarian search with less than the best possible result. Not only does online bibliographic searching save enormous amounts of time for the librarian, it also provides the ability to search exhaustively on complicated coordinate subject searches and retrieve citations that are highly relevant to the users' needs.

CD-ROM databases

A recent innovation for access to online databases and a variety of other reference sources is the CD-ROM capability that is rapidly gaining in popularity in a variety of large and small libraries. In order for the librarian to utilize this technology, a microcomputer and compact disk reader are required. Many publishers of abstracts and indexes are adopting this technology as an alternative means of providing their services. In some cases, vendors are converting existing databases to the CD-ROM format. A typical subscription to an indexing service on CD-ROM might include a compact disk version of the same indexing that is also available in print or online format, a menu-driven software package that enables one to search the indexing, and a regular schedule for updating the database. Such a subscription would then allow the librarian to search the indexing service in-house with no telecommunication connect charge, no royalty fee above the subscription fee, and no printing charge. The major advantage is the ability to have unlimited access to the indexing service without paying more than the prescribed subscription charge.

With online searching using telecommunication systems and current vendor fees, the more that a librarian searches, the more that is owed to the online vendor. With a CD-ROM search system, the cost per search decreases to the extent that the system is used. With a user-friendly CD-ROM MEDLINE database for example, both librarians and users can employ such a system on an almost constant basis if there is sufficient need, and the cost per search will continue to decrease as volume increases. One is also in control of the system because telephone problems and vendor downtime (times when the system is not available) are not considerations. One can search at three o'clock in the morning just as well as at noon. Some CD-ROM search software is not as sophisticated as that available through an online vendor and therefore some search capabilities may be limited. However, it may soon be difficult to distinguish between a CD-ROM and an online vendor version of the same database.

Integrated library systems

The concept of an integrated library system (ILS) was conceived early in the history of library automation utilizing the computer. This concept holds that with the creation of one complete master bibliographic file in machine-readable form, the library can utilize the information in this file to automate a large number of its functions. Information is recorded once for use by many. Thus, the master bibliographic file provides the basis for the online public access catalog (OPAC). It allows one to create circulation records for items that are checked out and it notes availability and return dates in the public catalog. For technical services it provides an on-order file, an in-process file, and all of the record systems needed for serials. Cataloging of materials builds upon data captured during the acquisition stage and ends with a complete bibliographic record with library location. When materials are removed from the collection, it is a simple matter to remove the electronic trail of an item from the master bibliographic file. Whenever necessary, a history file of past events from the master file can also be retained without effort. The principal advantages of an ILS include an up-to-date record of library holdings, immediate information on availability of items, and the potential for remote access from offices, laboratories, homes, and other sites. The accumulation and reporting of system statistics is also a major administrative advantage.

A number of major integrated library systems are being marketed nationwide, including OCLC's (Online Computer Library Center) LS2000, NOTIS (Northwestern Online Total Integrated System), CLSI (Computer Library Services, Incorporated), GEAC (GEAC Computer Corporation), and others. A specialized system that has been popular among medical libraries is the LIS (Library Information System) of Georgetown University. These systems all involve major investments in hardware and software. It is unlikely that the very small library would have the financial resources for such a major automation effort. However, there are already a number of microcomputer-based systems, and more of these will be available in the near future. As the software costs for such systems decrease, even the very small library will find that an ILS is a necessity. Such a system, functioning properly, may be the greatest time saver the librarian can employ. Because the installation of any automation system requires a large time investment for a library, the small library will probably best be served by adopting a "turnkey" system—a ready-made system that can be put in place with the least amount of effort and inconvenience. This approach limits the possibility of tailoring to meet local needs but it usually ensures changes and upgrades as the state of the art technology advances. System providers will continue to address common system user needs and provide improved versions of the ILS software.

Microcomputer applications software

Even though the cost of an ILS may currently be beyond the means of the small library, there are still a number of automation opportunities that should be investigated. The cost of a microcomputer is now well within the reach of almost any library. A variety of library software is being developed and made available either for free or for a very nominal cost. The librarian of the small library should use some of the sources cited in this work to identify specific software that might prove useful in a particular library setting. For example, a program to assist in journal check-in and routing may be readily available and save considerable time for the librarian. Programs for circulation, interlibrary loan, or production of catalog cards may also be worthwhile investments. The problem will not be in finding available programs, but rather in evaluating the various options available and selecting the one that will be most beneficial. State libraries, library associations, and various library systems and consortia may have individuals with expertise in some of the programs or an automation consultant whom the librarian can contact.

A number of workshops and national programs that may be helpful to the librarian are being offered on a regular basis. For example, the annual conference on Computers in Libraries (formerly, Small Computers in Libraries) is usually a good source for ideas, evaluation of applications software, and contacts with exhibitors who market library automation products. Sponsored by the publisher of *Computers in Libraries*, such conferences are usually a worthwhile investment in career development as well as a means of gaining practical advice.

Computer-assisted instruction

Computer-assisted instruction (CAI) has been used in libraries for at least twenty years. If the small library is part of an educational program, then the acquisition of CAI programs for use with microcomputers may well be part of the collection development policy. CAI will become increasingly complex as additional technology is coupled with the microcomputer to produce sophisticated and highly effective educational programs. For example, interactive CD-ROM programs that will make the user an active part of the learning process are currently being developed. This same technology can be coupled with laserdisk video players to produce a combination of interactive instruction with outstanding graphic capabilities. The small library of the future may devote more space to the use of microcomputers, video disk players, and CD-ROM than stack space for books and journals. Clearly, access to information in digital formats will play an important role in almost all types and sizes of libraries. Where the need for current, frequently updated information is greatest, such technology will be most in evidence.

Even if a small library does not have an educational function that can be served by CAI there are still instructional needs that can be effectively addressed by CAI. Many tutorial programs are already available that deal with access to information. For example, a CAI program on how to use an online database or even a printed abstracting or indexing service may be a highly effective means of bringing users and information together. If programming capabilities are among the librarian's skills, the librarian may create CAI programs on access to information within a specific library or subject discipline.

Artificial intelligence

The role of artificial intelligence (AI) in libraries is as yet unclear. It is likely that many of the online systems in use today may be improved through AI applications. For example, online literature searching could be improved by having searches refined through an interactive process and repeated searching until only highly specific citations are retrieved. Such citations might also be ranked in order of importance by some AI programs.

It is also likely that libraries will be providers of AI systems in much the same way that they provide access to online bibliographic and nonbibliographic systems today. In the field of medicine, for example, a number of so-called expert systems have already been developed and may soon become available for use. One such diagnostic system, DXplain, is already part of the computer network of the American Medical Association. In this system, the physician can input a patient's symptoms. The system then helps the physician by presenting a comprehensive picture of disease possibilities of which, in some cases, she might not be aware. Such consultative systems will undoubtedly be developed in a number of disciplines and library users will need to be aware of and have access to such systems. For example, an investment guide using AI applications might well be developed for the business community.

A useful and badly needed AI application in library and information science is one that would provide some means for information need identification, and search refinement and critique prior to the use of online or CD-ROM search systems. Such a program would enable a librarian or user to map out an appropriate search strategy and identify relevant search sources prior to beginning a search session. What is now an informal and often trial-and-error process could be a highly structured one that saves the librarian's or user's time and employs a more effective use of information resources with better information retrieval.

It is probably not an overstatement to say that automation in libraries, particularly computer use, has changed libraries more than any other event. It also seems clear that such changes are in a pioneer stage and that there will be an acceleration of technological enhancement of library capabilities. The librarian of the very small library may not be at the forefront of this development, but by keeping abreast of advances and seeking useful applications for particular library needs, the librarian will be able to provide better access to information resources than at any time in the past.

Suggested Readings

Allan, F. C., and J. M. Shields. "Automation Challenges of the 80's: What to Do Until Your Integrated Library System Arrives." *Special Libraries* 77 (Winter 1986): 15–19.

Bates, E. "Creating a Database for a Small Corporate Library NOMAD Bookcat." *Special Libraries* 74 (April 1983): 171–81.

Bierman, K. J. *Automation and the Small Library*. Chicago: American Library Association, 1982.

Bourne, C. P. "On-line Systems: History, Technology, and Economics." *Journal of the American Society for Information Science* 31 (May 1980): 155–60.

Burton, H. D. "Technology to Provide Excellence in Information Services." *Special Libraries* 78 (Winter 1987): 1–6.

Davis, R. M. "Where Will Technology Put the Library of the 21st Century?" *Bulletin of the Medical Library Association* 75 (January 1987): 1–6.

Dewey, P. *Software Packages to Use in Your Library: Descriptions, Evaluations, Practical Advice*. Chicago: American Library Association, 1987.

Dodson, C. "CD-ROMs for the Library." *Special Libraries* 78 (Summer 1987): 191–94.

Falk, H. *Personal Computers for Libraries*. Medford, N.J.: Learned Information, 1985.

Goldstein, C. M. "Integrated Library Systems." *Bulletin of the Medical Library Association* 71 (July 1983): 308–11.

Herther, N. K. "CD ROM Technology: A New Era for Information Storage and Retrieval?" *Online* 9 (November 1985): 17–28.

Hlava, M. M. K. "State of the Art 1985: Special Libraries/Online Technologies." *Special Libraries* 76 (Spring 1985): 121–25.

Kesner, R. M. "The Computer and the Library Environment: The Case for Microcomputers." *Journal of Library Administration* 3 (Summer 1982): 33–50.

Ketchell, D. S. "Online Searching By Microcomputer." *Bulletin of the Medical Library Association* 72 (October 1984): 370–72.

Kuntz, L. S. "An Integrated Library System from Existing Microcomputer Programs." *Special Libraries* 79 (Spring 1988): 115–21.

Lancaster, F. W., and L. C. Smith. "On-line Systems in the Communication Process: Projections." *Journal of the American Society for Information Science* 31 (May 1980): 193–200.

Nelson, N. M., ed. *Essential Guide to the Library IBM-PC*. Westport, Conn.: Meckler, 1986.

Summit, R. K., and C. T. Meadow. "Emerging Trends in the Online Industry." *Special Libraries* 76 (Spring 1985): 88–2.

Voos, Henry. "Telecommunications and Facsimile." *Special Libraries* 72 (April 1981): 118–21.

11   Space Management

Space management is of the utmost concern to the managers of most very small libraries. Of all the limited resources that such libraries face, none is perhaps so prevalent as the lack of suitable space. Even if the small library is successful in securing additional personnel, additional equipment, and additional sources of funding for collection development, the possibility of library expansion is often doubtful because additional space cannot be provided. In many organizations, space is at a premium and the library may have to continue to make do with what it has now; thus, the challenge is how to make the most effective use of the space that is available. This chapter examines ways in which space may be identified, made available, or better utilized to improve the library's performance.

The topic of space management is one that does not receive a great deal of attention in library literature. This may be because even though the problem is widespread, the nature of the problem is unique in each library setting. A solution that is useful to one library might not prove so to another. A library may find that its own growth—usually considered a good thing—has created severe space problems. Growth may mean that space is needed in one or more of the functional areas such as technical services, or it may mean that more user space is necessary in order to utilize the resources found in the library. Quite probably it involves a shortage of shelf space as well as a need for more space throughout the entire library. In addition, there may not be any private space in which the librarian can perform the many administrative tasks required in any library.

Any library can survive without increasing its space, but in order to continually move toward the goal of providing the best possible library service, space is an important consideration. The reality that confronts most librarians in very small libraries is the necessary assumption that no additional space will be forthcoming. The librarian's job then becomes that of finding the most creative and effective means of utilizing all available library space without dreaming of the day when the "new" library will eventually be built. For most small libraries that day will just not arrive.

A number of space-saving alternatives have been experimented with over the years. Each of these must be considered in light of the individual library's needs and evaluated for a particular library setting. No alternative should be ruled out until it has been carefully considered. Approaches that do not appeal to one personally may nevertheless work effectively. Some of the approaches to be considered are: saving on existing space by rearranging things, using shelving alternatives, changing library policy, and changing to microformats or other space-saving forms of information storage.

Rearranging library space

A variety of approaches exist for the rearrangement of existing library space. One must begin by examining how the space is currently being used or occupied. A good starting place is the circulation counter. This library mainstay often resembles the counter at the local pizza parlor. The process of charging and returning books does not require thirty square feet of counter space in a small library. Although such structures do serve as a focal point, virtually any piece of furniture located adjacent to the library entrance would also be easily identifiable as a circulation facility. A small desk might serve as a suitable replacement for the counter with a savings of close to twenty square feet. This extra room might then be converted to shelf space, user space, or space for some other function.

Similar approaches might be applied to the tables and chairs furnished for library users. Many libraries have acquired large tables capable of seating six or more individuals. Most library users, however, prefer to have a table to themselves and could just as easily use a smaller one. By replacing larger tables with smaller ones, it is possible to provide adequate seating while conserving floor space for other purposes. A reduction in the spacing between tables and chairs can also save space. Moving from six feet when chairs are back-to-back to only four feet may cause an occasional bump, but because the use of the small library is usually staggered throughout the day, there may be only a few periods when the library is crowded. Space can also be conserved between tables and chairs and points where they abut with shelving, counters, and walls.

Many librarians like to provide large, overstuffed chairs for relaxing based on the assumption that the library will receive greater use if it is "user friendly." While such an approach is worthwhile, other uses might be made of the space. Libraries often attempt to provide everything that users might want; perhaps it is more important to be able to display a few additional new journals rather than provide a comfortable lounge area.

Other library furnishings can be evaluated in a similar fashion. Vertical files are large and often take up a considerable amount of room. These may be very useful for storing ephemera, but how often is such material used? Can the library justify the space required to house an information resource that responds to only one question per day? per week? per month? The answer to this question may have to do with "just how much trouble would it be to find this information if these files were not physically present in the library."

Changing the shelving arrangements

Another approach to the space problem is to change the shelving arrangement within the library. Before undertaking this alternative, the collection should be thoroughly weeded.

One shelving alternative is to decrease aisle space in the stack area from thirty to thirty-six inches to as little as twenty-two inches. Most book trucks are approximately twelve to fourteen inches wide and they can move smoothly through narrowed aisles. It might be necessary to retrieve materials for individuals who cannot move easily through the tighter stacks. Persons in wheelchairs will have to be helped, and the librarian should be aware of local and federal regulations that might prevent such a shelf arrangement. In some cases, however, aisle reduction may be practical. It may be that space for wheelchair passage within the stack area is something the library cannot afford. Similar considerations might occur for any user if materials are to be placed in a nonuser area or if access is restricted by the need to use ladders, or other means of retrieving materials. The librarian will have to help in retrieving needed material.

The use of narrower shelves can also increase shelving space. Most libraries use nine-inch shelves. When shelves are arranged back to back, as is the case with double-faced library shelving, there is an additional two inches of "dead space" where the shelves back up to each other. Most books measure no more than seven inches from spine to fore edge, and approximately 95 percent of all books could fit on a seven-inch shelf. There would still be the same dead space for books that exceed the seven inches. Combined with narrower aisles, this arrangement may aid in compressing the stack area.

Another alternative is to add more shelves to each section of shelving and utilize the available space at the top and bottom of each shelving section. In a storage area or little used collection one might even place books on their fore edges and add more shelves. Inconvenience in shelving and possible damage to the spines of books makes this a less desirable approach. Shelves near the ceiling will require ladders or stools, and the potential for liability should be recognized. Use of lower shelves will mean that the candlepower for lighting may need to be increased so that titles and classification numbers can be read.

Special types of shelving also offer possibilities for increased storage capacity. One type consists of single- or double-faced units that slide back and forth or pull out from one or both sides of a book stack. Attached to uprights or to a wall that is capable of supporting significant amounts of weight, these units may resemble a series of drawers that pull out and slide back and forth to reveal additional storage drawers behind them. The librarian should check with an engineer and not accept advertising or a salesperson's word alone. All such shelving arrangements have some disadvantage, and with these units it is the inconvenience of moving elements around until the right drawer or shelf becomes accessible.

Additional shelving can also be placed on the ends of each range of shelving. This is the same as adding another section, but it cuts down on aisle space and makes it difficult to move around in the stacks. Users also need to be alerted to the continuation of the classification system or title arrangement as they move around the ends of the ranges.

A final type of so-called compact shelving uses single- or double-faced sections and the entire range moves perpendicularly on tracks or rails. This type may be either manually operated or motorized. It employs the principal that one aisle can serve for between four and twelve ranges. The aisle space is shared by moving the ranges back and forth until the aisle is in the correct position to retrieve the needed material. This approach makes maximum use of shelving space and is highly appropriate for the very small library. As with other shelving systems which greatly increase the concentration of weight as the collection is compacted, the load bearing capabilities of the library must be verified with an engineer. From the user's standpoint, the main disadvantage is that only one part of the classification scheme or alphabet is accessible at any one time, and to get to other places in the collection may first require moving the aisle.

Changing library policy

A radical move when space is at a premium might involve the elimination of user space altogether. The user would present an information request, preferably by telephone, and the library would respond by delivering the needed information for use someplace outside the library. If necessary, the information source would be returned to the library when the user was finished. This is certainly a feasible approach for the very small library, and it might result in far greater use of information than found in a conventional approach involving user space within the library. If the principal users of the library have their own offices and the library is conveniently located or delivery service is available, then they might prefer to use materials in places other than the library. In any case, most small special libraries probably need to provide seating for only a small fraction of the potential user group. A maximum of 10 percent of the total user group is suggested by Ahrensfeld and her coauthors. Just providing such user space, however, does not mean that library materials will be used within the library. If a decision is made to eliminate or greatly reduce the amount of user space within the library, then other factors relating to the circulation of materials, photocopy facilities, and response time to users' requests will have to be carefully evaluated to facilitate the use of materials outside the library. With less user space in the library there may be a need to have additional library staff to service information requests. As with any change, the public relations effect must be considered along with the need to inform users of the changes that are taking place.

Another alternative when the library faces the possibility of no additional space from any source is a policy of zero collection growth. This means that for every book that is added to the collection, one is removed. If the librarian is conscientious in weeding the collection, this alternative is untenable because all the books on the shelves have already been evaluated and need to be available for library users. Removing a book so that one may be added may solve the shelving problem, but there is no way of knowing whether the item removed or the one added will be critical to a future information need. Both books may need to be available, and this method precludes that possibility.

Changes in circulation policy

A change in circulation policy is an additional means of acquiring more space without any real modification to the physical library. This approach entails a policy that enables users to have library materials for an indefinite loan period. Most librarians, especially in very small libraries, are not overly concerned about always being able to see the materials that the library owns. The important thing is to be able to retrieve needed materials within a reasonable period of time when they are requested. Indefinite loan policies enable the library to utilize the shelving in the offices and laboratories that exist within the broader organization. Some of the materials not in use might just as well be in someone's office as occupying space on library shelves. One of the obvious disadvantages of this arrangement would be that everyone may decide to return borrowed materials to the library all at once. But as an expedient to a critical shelving problem, consider the library with twenty thousand volumes that only has space to shelve ten thousand volumes. Indefinite loan policies might help ease this situation without the extreme of a zero growth policy. This does involve an element of crisis management that some librarians might find too unpredictable.

Microforms and other storage formats

Microforms have long offered a potential for space savings in all types of libraries by compacting infrequently used material through photo reduction. For many years back files of journals, dissertations, and newspapers have appeared in such formats. Little actual dollar savings result from such conversion, but the space saved is notable. For example, many libraries are now housing technical report literature on microfiche. Even with the savings in shelf space, filing cabinets are needed to house these microfiche reports, and in a large academic library these materials may also create a space problem. This problem would increase a hundredfold, however, if paper copies were to replace the microfiche. For the very small library, any material that will be used infrequently but requires immediate access should be a candidate for conversion to micro format. Back files of important periodicals are a prime example. Some abstracting and indexing services also offer microform products and these might help conserve space. Access through online services might even eliminate the need for these microfilm back files or at least serve as a means of immediate access to earlier coverage of the journal literature.

Libraries appear to be on the verge of adopting many different technologies that provide for compact storage of information. Through the use of the videodisk and CD-ROM, it appears that the small library of the future will be able to store vast quantities of printed material in a digital format that also incorporates graphics. It is conceivable that a small library in the years ahead may well contain hundreds of thousands of volumes of material in a compact format all within a very small physical setting. Even if the materials are not physically present in the small library, there is little doubt but that they will be available through networking agreements. In the meantime, the critical lack of space faced by most libraries needs to be continually addressed.

Off-site storage of little used materials

Storage of materials outside the library proper is an attractive alternative to the zero growth concept. The very small library may have trouble finding a suitable storage space that provides security, convenient access, and environmental control. The storage area should be as close to the library as possible because the librarian will have to make at least occasional trips to the storage area. Off-site storage facilities (those built or rented for storage) are usually considered practical only for larger libraries, but the small library might be able to participate in a cooperative agreement with several local libraries that need to store little used materials. Book and journal collections in similar types of libraries frequently have an overlap in titles amounting to as much as 50 percent of the collection. Combined off-site storage would eliminate the need to retain more than one or two copies of the same title in order to meet the needs of all the cooperating libraries.

The major considerations of off-site storage are the cost of acquiring and maintaining the site, the inconvenience of transferring materials between the library and the storage site, and the required updating of library records. There is a hidden cost in the time and effort taken by library users and staff in identifying items for storage. If a storage facility is used, shelving arrangements can be made to accommodate the greatest number of books. Storage areas need not provide for browsing or convenient user access. In most cases, library users would not be permitted free access to the storage area. One of the best methods of maximizing storage capacity is to shelve books by size. Books are normally housed in three categories: quarto, folio, and everything else. By arranging books according to seven different sizes—folio, quarto, octavo, duodecimo, sixteenmo, twentyfourmo, and everything else—it may be possible to increase shelving capacity by as much as 25 percent over a random or mixed arrangement.

Housing other library operations

Housing the library's collection usually takes up most of the available space in the very small library, but nonuser areas for technical services and room for gifts and exchange processes are also important. It may be possible to find space for some of these activities outside the library proper. Space that does not have a high priority for other organizational activities can be used for many of the library's technical service operations. Even in the very small library, there may be occasional clerical or volunteer staff who perform some of these functions and their physical presence within the library itself is often not considered necessary. It may be possible to eliminate some of these functions by contracting them to a vendor or outside agent as when purchasing preprocessed books. As noted earlier, larger academic libraries may seek to contract for such business in order to maintain their resources and facilities. Similar consideration might be given to providing interlibrary loans, photocopies, and the exchange of materials through third parties so that the very small library does not have to devote floor space and staff to these functions.

When everything else has been tried, the librarian in a small library needs to be creative in finding additional floor space. How much space might be gained if the split leaf philodendron was moved to the company's front office? We all like to make our work environment more appealing, but when we run out of alternatives, what can we really do without in the library? Does anyone really use the beautiful globe on its free turning stand? Could the atlas serve just as well while taking up less space? A private office for the librarian provides a place for planning and administrative functions, but could that same space better serve the library if it were devoted to some other function? The choices may be difficult, but the alternatives should at least be examined.

When the librarian runs out of ideas, she should invite other librarians to come in and look around. It may be that a fresh way of looking at things is all that is needed to reveal additional space alternatives.

Even though the very small library may have little chance for additional space through renovation or new construction, the librarian should always look ahead five to ten years in addressing the long-range space needs of the library as well as acting on the space needs that occur on a day-to-day basis.

Suggested Readings

Cohen, A., and E. Cohen. *Designing and Space Planning for Libraries*. New York: R. R. Bowker, 1979.

Klein, M. S. "Space Utilization in Hospital Libraries with Space Shortages." *Bulletin of the Medical Library Association* 65 (January 1977): 63–65.

Montanelli, D. S. "Space Management for Libraries." *Illinois Libraries* 69 (February 1987): 130–38.

Myller, R. "Gaining Space by Creative Rearrangement of Library Areas." In Nygen, Karl, ed. "Library space planning." *Library Journal*, Special Report #1. New York: R. R. Bowker, 1976.

12 Evaluation of Library Services

Measuring goal attainment

Evaluation is the process of measuring the library's attainment of its stated goals. If specific performance measures or quantitative standards of performance are written for each objective, then measurement becomes a relatively easy task. Unfortunately, not all library operations can be readily quantified and thus measurement becomes less tangible. In many cases it is largely a subjective determination. Because of the extreme importance of the librarian's time in a small library, activity that does not lead to goal attainment is highly counterproductive. The following areas should receive attention in evaluating the library's performance: the scope, depth, and quality of the collection; the library's response time to all types of information requests; the accuracy of information provided in response to inquiries; the ease with which users may obtain materials and information; and the reasons why some requests are not filled.

As with most activities involved with running a small library, the above measurements will be largely dependent upon data gathered throughout the year. Measurements such as response time and the reasons why requests were not filled can be easily documented and tallied periodically. Other factors such as the quality of the collection, the accuracy of information provided, and the ease of access to information may be more difficult to quantify. In some cases the library users must directly provide the data upon which measurements will be based.

Evaluating the services

One of the best ways to involve library users in the evaluation process is to routinely ask for feedback as services are provided. For reference services this can be part of the form used to record the information request and the search process. It is probably better to solicit an evaluation at the time the service is provided simply because forms taken from the library or sent to the user to be filled in later seldom find their way back to the library. When this happens, the only responses may be from those who were highly pleased or greatly displeased with the library's performance. The disadvantage of asking for user evaluations immediately upon receiving the service is the reluctance of some individuals to be completely candid in the presence of the librarian. One way of overcoming this is to leave the form with the user at the time the service is provided and ask that they respond to the evaluation portion and drop the form in a box provided for that purpose before leaving the library.

In many libraries the provision of online bibliographic searches will be one of the principal activities of the librarian. Because of the increasing importance of this service to many library users and the amount of time it consumes, the librarian should attempt to verify its value. Again, evaluation by the user within the library may be the best way to ensure the receipt of such information; however, it may be necessary to mail the search results or wait until journal articles have been seen by the user (photocopied from the collection or obtained through interlibrary loan) before he or she can make an accurate assessment of the value of the search. One alternative is to note the user's immediate evaluation of the search result based on his or her judgment of the document surrogates (citations), then provide some subsequent means of follow-up evaluation after the user has had a chance to see the complete articles—perhaps as much as thirty days after the search was conducted.

In addition to evaluations obtained from library records and users, it is important that the librarian also seek information from people who do not use the library. The evaluation of the library and its services by nonusers is the "other side of the coin" and must be considered carefully in trying to measure library effectiveness. If only a small number of those who should use the library actually do, then even high marks in evaluation may not be very meaningful. The question to be answered is: "Why don't these individuals use the library?" Reliable answers can be very difficult to obtain in this area of evaluation. The best approach may be to solicit information through personal contacts where the issue can be placed in perspective. But because there is usually not enough time to contact nonusers personally, it may be necessary to gather such data from some central point within the organization. One way might be to place questionnaires on tables in the cafeteria and ask that they be filled out and deposited in a box placed there for that purpose. A questionnaire in the company newsletter may also be effective but it could be ignored or overlooked. One might distribute the questionnaire by placing a copy on the windshield of each car in the employee parking lot. This method may limit response because not all individuals drive to work. The value of the information derived from any of these methods will probably be improved if the responses to the questionnaire can be offered anonymously.

Evaluating the collection

Measurement of the less tangible aspects of library performance such as the quality of the collection may depend largely upon the opinions of library users. This information can be solicited as part of an ongoing user study or periodically as part of the evaluation process. It is useful to remember that evaluation instruments such as questionnaires, as with anything sent to library users, should be considered with regard to their public relations value. All forms should provide a professional image of the library and attempt to create goodwill. In addition to questionnaires seeking users' opinions, any quantitative means of measurement that is available should also be considered.

It may be possible to compare the library's collection to a similar collection that is already acknowledged for its quality, scope, and completeness. Some notable collections have had their catalogs reproduced in book form by the G. K. Hall Company and these are available in many libraries. There may be published bibliographies on topics of interest to a particular small library that can be checked against library holdings. A continuing analysis of requests that the library makes for interlibrary loans should provide an evaluation on an ongoing basis. Such evaluation should feed back into the acquisition process so that items that should be a permanent part of the collection are identified and subsequently ordered.

Another approach to collection evaluation is to select monographs and journal articles on subjects that are of concern to the users of the collection. By checking the bibliographies in these sources against the library's holdings, one can determine whether it would have been possible to write that particular work within this organization's library. For example, if a firm is doing research in health applications of laser technology, then key papers in this field should contain references to works that are available in the company library. This does not measure the overall quality of the collection, but it does indicate its value in a given area or for a particular topic.

One might also ask subject experts in the same organization to aid in evaluating the library's collection. Such individuals would ideally be active participants in the selection process, but even so, they may view the collection from a different perspective if asked to participate in a more comprehensive evaluation. Colleagues who manage other small libraries might also help in evaluation. For example, two hospitals with similar affiliations and teaching programs should have some common collection needs and a cross comparison of the collections might benefit both libraries.

More and more library consortia, systems, and cooperatives are becoming involved in collection analysis to determine subject scope and depth for member libraries. A conspectus or collection matrix is a necessary first step for meaningful cooperative collection development and resource sharing. In addition, the existence of such a conspectus might enable any small library to compare its collection on broad quantitative and qualitative measures with other similar collections.

Meeting library standards

Part of the evaluation process for any library is to consider how well the library measures up to available standards. Standards may be issued by a professional association, a state, or some other body concerned with performance criteria for certain types of libraries. The somewhat outdated standards of the Special Libraries Association are referred to in a number of places in this work. Public librarians should also be aware of the 1987 publication on output measures for public libraries issued by the American Library Association.

Some of the measures discussed in the ALA publication are frequently of concern to other types of libraries, and the ratios derived from data for these measures could well be used in a number of small library settings. The comparisons one might make from the output measures is fairly self-evident in the name of each measure. Listed here are the names of the measures. For further information on data sources, method of gathering data, amount of effort needed to gather needed data and time factors, please see the chapter bibliography.

Output measures:

Annual library visits per capita
Circulation per capita
In-library materials use per capita
Turnover rate (annual circulation as a percentage of holdings)
Title fill rate
Subject/author fill rate
Browsers' fill rate
Document delivery
Reference transactions per capita
Reference completion rate
Registrations as percentage of population
Program attendance per capita[1]

Evaluating library personnel

When there is more than one person working in the library, an additional type of evaluation is required. Staff performance, including that of volunteers, must be documented so that the librarian can determine whether or not the time invested in the additional personnel is worthwhile. There is a variety of opinions among managers concerning staff evaluations. There is also a wide range of measurement instruments. The important thing is to find some means of evaluation that is effective yet does not require a large expenditure of the librarian's time. The points to be evaluated are very similar to the measurements used to gauge library effectiveness as a whole. These are quality of work, response time, accuracy, attitude, dependability, and for personnel, loyalty. All of these attributes are important, but in a very small library, the personal qualities take on an added significance. It would appear that the smaller the size of the library staff, the greater the need for strong interpersonal skills on the part of library personnel. Such skills are evident not only to other staff members but to the library's users as well.

Self-evaluation

A personal type of evaluation in the small library should be the librarian's self-evaluation. It is likely that the librarian will receive a formal evaluation from his or her supervisor, but self-evaluation is a necessary part of the librarian's job as well. In most cases, the supervisor of the library will not have more than a limited knowledge of library operations; thus it is up to the librarian to make some type of informal evaluation of how well the job of librarian is being performed. Certain aspects of the librarian's performance are measured by the library's attainment of its objectives, but it would also be useful for the librarian to outline a few personal job-related objectives for each new year and then evaluate the attainment of these objectives periodically. For example, personal objectives might include greater participation in professional organizations, completion and publication of some library-related research, or greater visibility for the library outside the parent organization or institution.

There is a danger, probably greater than in larger libraries, that the librarian in the very small library will experience so-called "burnout." There is simply never enough time to get everything done and do things as thoroughly as one would like. The librarian in the small library must be highly committed to setting priorities and then pacing himself in accomplishing the needed tasks. The use of self-evaluation will at least allow the librarian a chance for reflection and possibly, redirection.

User comments

Many libraries, regardless of size, find that the use of a suggestion box or comment cards can elicit meaningful user input and play an effective part in library public relations. Comments cards are help-ful because they require a response from the librarian and when posted, such concerns and answers are informative to other library users. A sample comment card is included at the end of this chap-ter. Cards can be displayed at the circulation counter and users may help themselves and then deposit them in a box provided for that purpose. The librarian should make sure that such complaints, suggestions, and concerns are answered promptly and posted in a conspicuous place in the library. All comments deserve an answer no matter how inconsequential or uninformed they may be. On oc-casion, a useful suggestion will lead to improvement of the library's collection or services. The librarian might be tempted to infer that a lack of user comments is correlated to a positive evaluation for the library, but he should guard against placing too much con-fidence in such an inference.

Appendix

Sample Comment Card

Suggestion or Complaint
(Compliments, too, are accepted)

_____

_____

_____

Name (optional) _____ Date_____

_____

Library Reply

_____

_____

_____

Name _____ Date_____

Response will be posted.

Note

1. N. A. Van House et al., *Output Measures for Public Libraries: A Manual of Standardized Procedures*, 2d ed. (Chicago: American Library Association, 1987), 189.

Suggested Readings

Brown, M. K. "Library Data, Statistics, and Information." *Special Libraries* 71 (November 1980): 475–84.
Chen, Ching-chih. *Quantitative Measurement and Dynamic Library Service.* Phoenix: Oryx Press, 1978.
Childers, T. A. "Test of Reference." *Library Journal* 105 (April 15, 1980): 924–28.
Gore, D. "Mischief In Measurement." *Library Journal* 103 (May 1, 1978): 933–37.
Lancaster, F. W. *Measurement and Evaluation of Library Services.* Washington, D.C.: Information Resources Press, 1977.
Manthey, Teresa, and J. O. Brown. "Evaluating a Special Library Using Public Library Output Measures." *Special Libraries* 76 (Fall 1985): 282–89.
Martyn, J., and F. W. Lancaster. *Investigative Methods in Library and Information Science.* Washington, D.C.: Information Resources Press, 1981.
McClure, C. R., and Betsy Reinfsnyder. "Performance Measures for Corporate Information Centers." *Special Libraries* 75 (July 1984): 193–204.
Pings, V. M. "Reference Services Accountability and Measurement." *RQ* 16 (Winter 1976): 120–23.
Spencer, C. C. "Random Time Sampling with Self-Observation for Library Cost Studies: Unit Costs of Reference Questions." *Bulletin of the Medical Library Association* 68 (January 1980): 53–57.
Stevenson, C. G. "Checklist for Review and Evaluation of Technical Libraries." *Special Libraries* 58 (February 1967): 106–10.
Strain, P. M. "Evaluation by the Numbers." *Special Libraries* 73 (July 1982): 165–72.
Tagliacozzo, R. "Estimating the Satisfaction of Information Users." *Bulletin of the Medical Library Association* 65 (April 1977): 243–49.
Van House, N. A. et al. *Output Measures for Public Libraries: A Manual of Standardized Procedures.* 2d ed. Chicago: American Library Association, 1987.
Warden, C. L. "User Evaluation of a Corporate Library Online Search Service." *Special Libraries* 72 (April 1981): 113–17.
Weinrach, E. L. "Self-evaluation." *Catholic Library World* 47 (December 1975): 220–23.
White, G. T. "Quantitative Measures of Library Effectiveness." *Journal of Academic Librarianship* 3 (July 1977): 128–36.

13 Public Relations

Public relations is a recurring theme throughout this work because it is crucial to the success of the librarian in the very small library. Academic and school libraries will probably continue to exist and may even grow regardless of how they are perceived by their users. Public libraries represent ideals that are held sacred by society and these ideals do not change even though the library may have no positive public relations. Most public libraries will continue to exist but may suffer setbacks through no fault of their own because they are often funded from tax bases and their prosperity may be controlled by forces over which they have little direct influence.

For special libraries, however, and especially the very small library where any decrease in financial support would be devastating, the importance of positive public relations cannot be overemphasized. Without strong support from the principal user group, a small special library is constantly in danger of extermination. This is why special librarians are so well-versed in the concept of continually "selling" the library. While the importance of public relations created through other library functions has already been discussed, there are additional direct and indirect ways in which the image of the library can be affected. This chapter will look at some of the areas that need special attention if the very small library is to create and maintain a positive public image.

How the library represents itself

Outside appearance plays a major role in the public's perception of the library. Most small libraries have little if any say about this aspect. However, librarians may make suggestions to management for improvements if they are needed. Certainly the librarian should be concerned about the sign that identifies the library. This sign should convey a professional image. If we want the library to be heavily used, why hide the fact that it exists? Although proper utilization of floor space inside the library has already been discussed, it does bear repeating that this is a very important part of the image the library presents to its users. Hazards, mazes, and physical complications all promote a negative public image.

Signs, displays, exhibits, and bulletin boards

Each of these aspects of library operation has a public relations function in addition to other objectives. Signs and graphics used inside the library need a professional touch. Consultation and printing services are often available within the parent organization. Library users need a focal point upon entering the library and they need to know where to go for assistance. If these areas are not obvious, signs may help. The overuse of signs (as with the obtrusive presence of a librarian) can create the opposite of the desired effect. Signs should never be used excessively; they should be simple and used only when necessary.

The essential difference between displays and exhibits is intent. Displays are intended to inform library users, exhibits have a more ambitious educational objective. Displays should be changed every few weeks. Uniqueness is important if library users are to focus on the message that the library has to convey. Displays may feature anything that is of interest to the organization's employees. This can involve company products or activities, community-related activities, or something more directly connected to the library, such as library materials on a particular topic. Many health sciences libraries, for example, display works by the most recent recipients of the Nobel Prize for Medicine and Physiology at the time the award is announced each year. A music library might want to highlight the anniversary of the birth of a famous composer by using a short-term display of musical scores and books devoted to the artist. In both cases, the principal function of the display is to inform.

Displays prepared by the library might even be placed in areas outside the library. A display of library materials in the cafeteria or in a staff lounge could produce public relations benefits.

Most libraries have some means for mounting exhibits that can remain in place for weeks or even months at a time. It is not likely that the librarian of the very small library will have much time to prepare exhibits. Should volunteer help be available, this is a project that can be assigned that will require little supervision and may tap the artistic talents and imagination of the person involved. To be effective, exhibits must be of a high quality or the public relations value is defeated and may even be reversed.

Bulletin boards are a good way of providing a current awareness service that might otherwise be lacking in a small library. Notices about meetings, changes in library hours and/or policies, book jackets, and responses to users' suggestions for change or improvement can all be posted on a bulletin board with the result being positive public relations for the library. In order for this to occur, a few rules must be followed: (1) rotate the materials on the board with some frequency (date all materials before posting); (2) have some plan of organization for the board and prevent clutter; (3) be aware of positioning to catch a person's eye for the most important material; (4) schedule the clearing and arranging of the board so that it is done on an regular basis.

Print media

With no more than a good typewriter and photo duplication facilities the librarian can effectively produce a variety of publications. Many of the forms used for library operations can be done in this fashion as well. It is important from a public relations standpoint that such forms be as clear and simple as possible in both message and format and that they convey a professional image. Microcomputer desk-top publishing programs now greatly enhance local production options at a relatively small cost.

The library bulletin is considered an extra service by many librarians. This is usually a monthly or bimonthly publication that contains news of the library about staff, collection, facilities, and services. It may also include a list of recent acquisitions. If one pictures this as a public relations document, then the content will probably be quite different from that used in a publication for library staff. A publication that is oriented toward public relations can become a selling device for the library's services, not just a miniature monthly report for the librarian.

Only those items that provide information needed by users should be included in a public relations bulletin. All material should be written with the goal of creating a positive image for the library. For example, short lists of more important acquisitions are preferable to long lists that attempt to include everything acquired. The provision of one- or two-line annotations can also greatly improve the readability and usefulness of such lists. Noting that a particular book is a new edition previously issued under another author's name can be highly important to some of the readers of the bulletin. When preparing such a bulletin, concentrate on what the library users want to know, not just what the librarian thinks is important.

If the audience for the bulletin is other librarians, then the content will probably be entirely different. Items such as forthcoming library meetings, reports of continuing education activities, methods of providing new user services, resource sharing information, and library performance measures will appeal most to other librarians. Some items will be appropriate for publication in a bulletin directed at either group. Even with a well-produced library bulletin, the intended public relations effect may not be achieved if it does not appear on a regular schedule. Users should always know when to expect the next installment, and it should be issued in a timely fashion.

Distribution of a library bulletin could have a negative financial impact on a small library if copies are mailed to individuals. Postage quickly adds up to more than the cost of paper and printing for the bulletin. If cost is a consideration, distribution may be limited only to those that can be reached through the organization's internal mailing system.

Acquisition lists by themselves may be a useful public relations tool for the very small library, but some selectivity should be exercised and titles should be annotated, if possible. At the very least, titles should be grouped by subject so that users do not have to go through the entire list in order to identify books or other documents that might be of interest. Short acquisition lists can be especially effective if the materials are new and of central interest to the organization. Frequently, the acquisition list is the only contact that some of the library's potential users have with the library.

If the list is discontinued, the library ceases to exist for these individuals.

Company newsletters or other publications of the parent organization may also provide an avenue for library public relations. The librarian may be able to furnish a regular column in the organizational publication. As is true for the library bulletin, the purpose should be to promote the library within the organization. Frequently, the editor of such a publication has sole control over content and style. If the librarian thinks that these are not appropriate or of a high quality, then a decision to publish a library bulletin instead might be more appropriate. The use of the organization's publication, however, will be less costly in terms of the librarian's time and for that reason may be a more attractive alternative for some librarians.

Articles about the library, its services, plans, etc., may be suitable for publication in the professional literature of librarianship or in the literature of the subject disciplines served by the library. For example, many hospital librarians have published articles about library services in state medical journals. When writing for a library journal, the content of the article should appeal to other librarians. This will have positive public relations value if the librarian makes sure that members of the organization know that the company and its library were discussed in a particular journal. If literature of the discipline is used as the means for publication, then the article may be more of a selling device for library services. In either case, reprints of article should be widely distributed within the organization.

It may be possible for some small libraries to have a local newspaper publish a feature story on the library and the services it provides. It is certainly worth a try if the library and its collection and services are unique. Becoming acquainted with staff members of the local newspaper, perhaps through a newspaper librarian, is always a good idea even if no library-related publications are forthcoming.

Presentations about the small library made to one's colleagues at professional meetings can be used to create positive public relations. Because there is no actual publication involved in most cases, the librarian should make sure that top officials within the organization are aware of the presentation. The librarian can achieve this by putting a notice in the library bulletin or by sending a copy of the program to company officials.

Some larger libraries have utilized audiovisual productions as a means of publicizing the library and its services. For the small library, such an effort is probably not practical; however, there may be an audiovisual department within the organization that can include the library in some of its productions. If so, then this could be an effective means of selling the library to its public.

Reaching out to users

Library communications often provide the only contact that some users and prospective users have with the library. Forms used by patrons within the library or those sent to users or potential users should convey the professional image of the library. The wording in such literature should communicate the service capability of the library and never display negativity or threaten action for inappropriate behavior. Although there does come a point in the collection process for lost materials when this last guideline may no longer apply, the librarian should carefully consider whether extensive methods to collect small amounts offset the negative impression that is created.

Other direct communications involve face-to-face interaction between the user and library staff. Negative attitudes are easily conveyed through word choice, tone of voice, and body language during such contacts. Failure to speak is often as damaging to public image as what may be said. This also applies to telephone conversations where the library user has even fewer signs to interpret. A remark that might normally create a favorable impression when accompanied by the librarian's smile may have the opposite affect over the telephone.

The librarian is usually not able to spend much time away from the library; however, an effort should be made to meet library users and potential users in their work environments. This means visiting offices, laboratories, and other facilities, and attending functions sponsored by the parent institution. The importance of the appearance of the librarian at company social events and other organizational activities cannot be stressed enough. There are a number of other ways that the librarian can take the public relations campaign directly to the potential users of the library. One of these is through membership on organization committees. Top management has to be educated about the importance of having the librarian sit in on the meetings of all planning committees whose decisions will have an impact upon future library development.

Membership on other types of committees will increase the visibility of the library and help the librarian to better understand how the organization functions.

One problem that can arise is that the librarian of the very small library may not have additional staff to run the library during absences. This will be the case with many activities that take the librarian away for either short or long periods. In most organizations it should be possible to provide access to the library during the librarian's absence without any undue trauma. See chapters 4 and 5 for information on how to plan for library access when the librarian is not available.

The librarian should consider volunteering for assignments that will put him or her in contact with many of the individuals in the organization. For example, as coordinator for the company's United Way effort or other charitable drives, the librarian can meet many of the library's potential users. The library's public relations can be enhanced under such circumstances.

Reaching individuals who never use the library may be one of the most difficult aspects of a public relations program. Wandering the halls, dropping into offices, or making the rounds in the cafeteria are all informal ways of meeting people within the organization, but the problem for the librarian of the very small library is finding the time to leave the library. The organization's internal mail system can also bring library information into contact with virtually all employees. A special library open house might also serve as an attraction for nonusers to find out what is going on. Because most employees of an organization are available sometime during the day at the work establishment, opportunities for contact are numerous.

Library support groups

Support groups are commonly identified with public libraries; special libraries in the corporate world would be least likely to have such a group as "the friends of the library." Even so, the use of library committees or library boards can generate a positive public image for the library as members become better informed about library services and needs. The role of any such group, whether it is a committee or a friends group, is to support the policies and decisions of the librarian. The group should be led, indirectly, by the librarian and serve the needs identified by the librarian. It is in no way meant to run the library.

Through the careful use of support groups, a librarian can strengthen the role of the library within an organization. For some small libraries, the extension of support groups outside the organization to the community will be quite appropriate. For example, the library of an art gallery might well have a friends of the library group made up of individuals from all walks of life. By promoting library programs, supporting acquisitions, and conducting fundraising campaigns and programs, these groups can do much to provide positive public relations for the library. Even if the library is not in a position to foster the formation of its own support group, there may be other support groups within the broader organization that would be glad to include the library in promotional activities.

The librarian of the very small library must constantly be aware of the importance of positive public relations for the library, for its very existence may well depend upon how much support the library can muster in a time of crisis. If the librarian has paid close attention to the public relations aspects of everything the library does, then support should be forthcoming.

Suggested Readings

Crookston, M. E. "Public Relations for the Special Library." *Special Libraries* 55 (May/June 1964): 283–85.

Fredericksen, R. B., and J. A. Thompson. "The Suggestion Card As an Alternative To the Suggestion Box." *Bulletin of the Medical Library Association* 68 (April 1980): 244–46.

Jones, C. L. "Substitute a Suggestion Book for Your Box." *Bulletin of the Medical Library Association* 65 (July 1977): 386–88.

Kohn, R., and K. Tepper. *You Can Do It: A PR Skills Manual for Librarians.* Metuchen, N.J.: Scarecrow Press, 1981.

Leatherbury, M. C., and R. A. Lyders. "Friends of the Library Groups In Health Sciences Libraries." *Bulletin of the Medical Library Association* 66 (July 1978): 315–18.

Lewis, R. F. "The Role of Exhibits in a Medical School Library." *Special Libraries* 49 (March 1958): 125–28.

Parker, S. M., and H. R. Purtle. "A Guide to the Planning and Development of Exhibits for Medical Libraries." *Bulletin of the Medical Library Association* 46 (July 1958): 335–43.

Social Science Group/Washington, D.C. Chapter. *A Sampler of Forms for Special Libraries*. New York: Special Libraries Association, 1982.

Zachert, M. J., and R. V. Williams. "Marketing Measures for Information Services." *Special Libraries* 77 (Spring 1986): 61–70.

Zinn, N. W. "Exhibits in Health Sciences Libraries." *Bulletin of the Medical Library Association* 72 (April 1984): 193–97.

14 Cooperation Among Libraries

Cooperation among librarians has long been a popular topic in the library literature. Until recent years, most cooperative efforts centered on the lending of materials through interlibrary loan. Today, cooperation is a concept that may involve extensive document delivery systems, joint acquisition programs, participation in bibliographic utilities, exchange of duplicate materials, consortium development, and any number of networking agreements or arrangements. Cooperation may be formalized in contracts or based on the continuance of informal practices often developed over the years.

Cooperation in the sharing of resources has been the mainstay of special librarianship since 1906, when John Cotton Dana founded the Special Library Association (SLA). Some of the association's first projects were to identify library resources, thus making them available to other librarians. Much of this early cooperation was informal in nature and any system that eliminated paperwork for the librarian of the small library was encouraged. A willingness to serve one another has proven to be one of the principal benefits that members of associations such as SLA have derived from the personal contacts established through association activities.

In recent years, networking on a national and international level has created a more formal mechanism for the sharing of resources among libraries. Networking agreements have given very small libraries access to a wider range of resources and enabled them to take advantage of standardized bibliographic records. The spinoff from many of these computer-based networks has been greater accessibility to a wider variety of information and elimination of much duplicative work within each individual library. In exchange for such benefits, the small library is faced with certain equipment, training, maintenance, and operating costs that tend to remain constant or exhibit normal cost of living increases from one budget period to the next. By participating in cooperative ventures, much of the work of acquiring, processing, and analyzing information for retrieval can be accomplished in far less time. This frees the librarian for the important work of providing reference services to the library's users.

Interlibrary loan and document delivery

Interlibrary loan (ILL) refers to the sharing between libraries of materials that must be sent either through the mail or by some sort of delivery service. This involves materials that are actually "loaned" to the borrowing library and that, in most cases, are to be returned. This is the practice that is most commonly used for books.

Because journal literature plays such an important role in information dissemination for most disciplines, the use of document delivery[1] is becoming more common. With this system, articles are photocopied (in compliance with the copyright law) and mailed or sent by telefacsimile to the "borrowing" library, which is not required to return the copies.

Superimposed upon this traditional borrowing-lending pattern has been the advent of document delivery vendors who usually utilize existing library collections (such as large academic libraries) to fill document requests from libraries and others. Such services are profit-oriented businesses. Vendors provide one alternative to the library in need of an article for which interlibrary loan is not possible or would result in a copyright violation. In many cases vendors also provide a means for automatic ordering in conjunction with the use of online databases. This makes for quicker service than possible by means of traditional interlibrary loan.

In the past, librarians attempted to provide for 100 percent of their users' needs through in-house collections and services. As libraries evolve, they are moving toward the use of access-based services where materials are acquired for use only if and when they are needed. These materials do not normally become part of the "borrowing" library's collection. It seems likely that the very small library will want to move in this direction as the transferal of documents from remote locations becomes more timely and cost effective.

In order for interlibrary loan to work effectively, one must be able to identify the holdings of other libraries. A spinoff of many automation projects has been to make bibliographic records widely available through union lists and bibliographic utilities such as the Online Computer Library Center (OCLC). Union lists are usually monographs, updated with some frequency, that identify the serial and/or book holdings of individual libraries. A number of libraries may join together in producing a union list for the benefit of all participating libraries. Bibliographic utilities can provide location information for serials and books input by participating libraries and, in some cases, an interlibrary loan system to facilitate the exchange of information can also be part of such a utility. Lists and utilities conserve the librarian's time and allow quicker access to materials for library users. OCLC is one of the best known of the bibliographic utilities for these purposes, but other more specialized sources are also available such as SERHOLD of the National Library of Medicine.

Some automated systems for document delivery provide for automatic routing of interlibrary loan requests among libraries identified through a profile supplied by the borrowing library. OCTINET and DOCLINE are two such systems. Information on such systems and on union lists is widely available in library literature. The time saved by such systems can be significant for the small library and this will be the case increasingly as the library becomes more oriented toward access-based information.

Once library holdings have been identified, then local access to material is highly important. The time saved by acquiring an item within one's own community has been the motivation behind much consortium development. A consortium is a group of local libraries that have joined together and agreed to borrow and lend library materials among themselves. This provides a basis for informal loan arrangements that can eliminate much of the time-consuming paperwork of document delivery. Only when local resources have been exhausted are members of the consortium to seek outside sources for loan fulfillment.

One of the great advantages of the consortium agreement is that it takes some of the pressure off the larger libraries that often lend large amounts of materials but borrow much less frequently. When they do borrow materials, it is usually from large libraries with unique items that they themselves do not own. If anything is going to bring about the end of the traditional interlibrary loan system in this country, it is probably this imbalance between lending and borrowing libraries because the sharing of materials ties up increasing amounts of the larger libraries' resources.

Some libraries have already resorted to expensive pricing systems to address this issue and more are likely to follow. Small libraries should look for ways of improving local resource sharing so that the only demands made on larger libraries are for materials that are clearly beyond the scope of, and not available from, smaller libraries.

The cost of interlibrary loan has often been presented as a mystery. Several studies have produced a figure ranging from $5 to $15 per transaction, but if careful pricing of all factors associated with each transaction were documented, the actual cost could be substantially higher. In an inefficient ILL system, the expense of operation could be equal to that of purchasing the needed material and processing it into the collection. Costs can be passed on to library users, but whether one chooses to do this or not, consortia, union lists, and automated systems should be employed to provide the most efficient system possible. A hidden cost, but probably the most important consideration, is the time that the user must wait until the needed material is available. This certainly justifies the use of telefacsimile service where, for most journal articles, exact duplicates of original materials can be transmitted between libraries within a matter of minutes. As this equipment and other technology improves (such as full-text computer-stored journals for downloading to a borrowing library), a substantial move toward access-based services should occur. The very small library will benefit greatly from these developments.

Cooperative acquisitions

Cooperative acquisition programs provide another way in which the very small library can obtain access to expanded information resources. By agreeing to acquire materials on certain subjects or from certain publishers and make them available to other libraries in exchange for materials they have agreed to purchase, the individual library's holdings are expanded to include the combined holdings of the cooperating libraries. This saves each library from having to house all the resources its users might want to consult. Such agreements have worked best when the participating libraries are located in the same general vicinity. However, with improved means of conveying information from one location to another, future agreements may be just as effective extended over vast geographic areas. For further discussion of cooperative acquisitions, see chapter 6.

Library networks

In addition to consortium agreements, most small libraries will have access to other types of networking arrangements. "Networking" is often used as a general term in place of cooperation. It is really more specific in that networking implies a greater degree of formalization among libraries as they share in the creation and use of network resources. Such formalization is often imposed by contractual agreements and extensive operating protocols. Some networks are highly structured, such as the Regional Medical Library Program of the National Library of Medicine, which serves virtually all health sciences libraries in this country. Other networks may be less visible, such as a group of libraries that has established a cooperative tradition of working together for the good of the group. The consortium is one type of network and may be highly structured or loosely organized. Theoretically, all libraries in this country comprise the total network of libraries. General library guidelines, such as the American Library Association National Interlibrary Loan Code available from the association, tend to add varying degrees of structure to this network.

Some networks have evolved from serving specialized purposes into broader based agreements. For example, in some states, public library networks have expanded to involve a mix of public, academic, special, and school libraries. The librarian of the very small library should explore opportunities within the local community and state for participation in mixed networks. Other network opportunities within specialized library associations or special disciplines may also be beneficial.

Large regional or national cooperative ventures may also be of direct benefit to the small library. Organizations such as AMIGOS (Amigos Bibliographic Council), SOLINET (Southeastern Library Network), and PALINET (Pennsylvania Area Library Network) can provide access to multiple services including bibliographic utilities such as OCLC and RLIN (Research Libraries Information Network). Although the librarian in the small library may not be able to attend network meetings, participation can still be valuable and some other means of providing input should be devised. Networks may also receive discounts for accessing online databases, provide library records in machine-readable format, and offer an extensive array of continuing education activities.

Librarians interested in learning of networking opportunities in their areas should contact their state libraries, professional associations, and talk to librarians with similar interests.

The future

The future for the very small library appears to be highly encouraging. More and more, organizations have identified the need for information as crucial to their operations. The librarian, information officer, or whatever name is chosen, must be able to identify information needs and then link these with information resources. Communities are also continuing to recognize the need for public libraries, even if they fall into the very small category. It is encouraging that such libraries continue to prosper and receive a share of the tax dollar despite increasing competition from highly sophisticated forms of recreation and entertainment.

It is quite likely that some very small libraries of the future may consist of little more than an office with equipment to access electronic information networks provided on local, regional, national, and international bases. The application of videodisk technology coupled with digital disk storage of information may mean that such libraries will virtually be able to store the complete text of the world's entire knowledge base in a relatively small space. A similar prediction was made by Vannevar Bush in an *Atlantic Monthly* article in 1945. Now, however, the technology to make his "memex" concept a reality is available and coming within acceptable cost parameters.

As information technology advances, libraries will benefit most directly by being part of a larger, formalized network that provides access to vast amounts of published and unpublished data. Linked information systems will be common within and between institutions. The integrated library system is already a reality for some libraries, and soon this system will be connected to other systems, providing virtually immediate access to all types of information regardless of where it is located.

One side effect of this development is that it will be necessary to protect the privacy and rights of individuals, and provide information to those who need it but do not have the funds to pay for it. Information will come to be regarded as a natural resource to be nurtured and protected. As in the past, much of the responsibility for marketing and disseminating information will fall upon the library. Because of the changing nature of libraries in the years ahead, it is likely that there will be more very small libraries than all other types of libraries combined. Despite the physical size of these libraries, their capabilities for information retrieval will be far beyond those of most large libraries today.

Cooperation through networking will continue to increase in importance as we move toward the next century. Libraries of all types and sizes must not lose sight of the fact, however, that the success of networking will depend upon the willingness of each individual institution to finance its own share. Cooperation does not mean "free." Even very small libraries must expect to reimburse network partners when appropriate so that continued access to needed materials will be assured.

Note

1. Document delivery is used to denote the use of photocopies in lieu of sending the original journal issue to the borrowing library. Document delivery frequently means that the borrowing library pays for the photocopy and is not required to return it to the lending library. Document delivery also means the role of the library in providing documents to its users. With the popularity of online bibliographic searching, many libraries have adopted document delivery policies to ensure that citations retrieved in searches are photocopied and delivered to the requesting user.

Cited Literature

Bush, Vannevar. "As We May Think." *Atlantic Monthly* 176 (January 1945): 101–108.

Suggested Readings

Gallimore, C. R., and R. R. Martin. "Holder of Record: A Cooperative Health Sciences Journal System in a Hospital Library Network." *Bulletin of the Medical Library Association* 68 (July 1980): 271–73.

Hill, L. L. "Issues in Network Participation for Corporate Librarians." *Special Libraries* 76 (Winter 1985): 2–10.

Robinson, B. M. "The Role of Special Libraries in the Emerging National Network: Critical Issues." *Special Libraries* 72 (January 1981): 8–17.

Glossary

Approval plan.   A method used by monograph vendors to supply regular shipments of books matching a library's profile. From each shipment, monographs are selected for purchase by the librarian; those not selected are returned to the vendor.

Basic Unit Cost (BUC).   A computation employed in performance budgeting whereby all direct costs for salary, supplies, equipment, rent, etc., plus indirect costs or overhead are used to calculate the per item cost for a library service or product, e.g., the cost of circulating one book.

Carrel.   An individual study table used by library patrons.

CD-ROM.   Compact Disk-Read Only Memory is an electronic storage medium in the form of a 5″ compact disk. Used with a CD-ROM reader and microcomputer, this technology allows inhouse use of databases without the need for telecommunications.

Collation.   A physical examination of materials received for addition to the library involving a page by page review to determine any publishing irregularities.

Collection development levels.   A group of designations for the degree of collection development activity; broken down by subject or type of materials, proceeding from most to least inclusive: Comprehensive, Research, Study, Basic, and Minimal.

Collection Development Policy (CDP).   A written statement describing the basis for acquiring materials to be added to the collection. Includes scope, depth, languages, time periods, etc. May also include policies for gifts, weeding, and the allocation of funds.

Computer memory.   Memory houses software (programs) controlling the hardware and applications being used. Microcomputers incorporate internal and hard disk memory.

Computer terminal.   A device for communicating with a computer. Formerly, "dumb" terminals were prevalent, but could be used only for searching and printing. Now microcomputers are replacing most dumb terminals, and can run programs and download and manipulate data.

Consortium.   A cooperating group of libraries consenting to voluntarily provide resources and services for the good of the group and to meet needs of individual libraries.

Conspectus.   A cooperative collection development tool listing the holdings of each participating library's collection by classification number or subject.

Content analysis.   A user study methodology by which existing records are examined to determine information needs and use.

Cooperative collection development program.   An acquisition program in which a number of libraries agree to identify library holdings collectively and attempt to build library collections based on both the collective and individual needs of the cooperating libraries.

Current awareness service.   A library service designed to alert users to information sources that might be of interest. Users select pertinent items from those highlighted by the service.

Database.   A file of related information elements containing bibliographic or non-bibliographic records, now commonly available online via computer.

Deposit account.   The requirement by some providers of publications and information products or services that a predetermined amount be deposited by the library against which future orders will be deducted.

Diary study.   A user study methodology by which individuals record their individual information needs and the means by which these needs were met during some established time period.

Digital.   A type of coding that uses a base-2 numbering system, which records data as either "0" or "1" and electronically stores this in a digital computer.

Downloading.   A process whereby portions of online databases are copied on the library's microcomputer from databases accessed through telecommunications.

Dummies.   Location markers placed on shelves in libraries to indicate that the item normally housed in that location is located somewhere else.

Electronic record.   Data elements for library materials recorded in digital format.

Fill rate.   Refers to the number of interlibrary loan requests that a library is able to complete through provision of the material needed or a photocopy.

Fulltext.   Describes electronic databases that provide the entire document.

Hardware.   The physical items of computer or audiovisual equipment that facilitate the use of various databases and media.

Hygienic factors.   According to the management theory of Frederick Herzberg, these are factors that influence employees' job dissatisfaction. Factors influencing job satisfaction are called "motivators."

Information transfer.   A term describing the entire process through which information is created, acquired, processed, disseminated, and utilized to produce new information which may add to or replace existing information and thereby move into the continuous information transfer cycle.

Integrated Library System (ILS).   A computer-based system in which a master bibliographic file of the library's holdings is used for various library operations and by patrons.

ISBN.   The International Standard Book Number that serves as a unique identifier for each book published.

ISSN.   The International Standard Serial Number that serves as a unique identifier for each serial published.

Jobber.   See "Vendor."

Library guide.   A library publication describing library policies, services, and facilities. Intended for distribution to potential library users.

Microfiche.   A unitized photographic medium on which reduced images of documents are stored for access by library users by means of a microfiche reader. Standard fiche size is 4" x 6".

Microfilm.   A continuous photographic medium on which reduced images of documents are stored for access by library users using a microfilm reader. The standard format is 16mm.

Online.   The means of accessing databases via computer terminals using telecommunication networks to link the library with the desired database.

Photoduplication.   The reproduction of library materials using any of the various means of duplication involving xerography or telefacsimile.

Pretest. The practice of selecting a small subset of those to whom a questionnaire or other method of data collection will be applied to determine and correct any problems with the data collection methodology.

Random sampling. A method used in research to select a sample that will be representative of the whole. Randomizing the selection process eliminates bias through disproportionate representation.

Ready reference. That phase of reference work devoted to providing brief, factual information to users' inquiries. The time spent in finding the answer is usually limited to a few minutes.

Return rate. The percentage of books that are returned to the vendor as part of an approval plan.

Selective Dissemination of Information (SDI). A type of awareness service in which information sources are matched against an individual user's profile and matched items are brought to the user's attention.

Serials. A generic term for any of the variety of publications that are issued on some regular basis and are intended to continue indefinitely. Includes: periodicals, journals, magazines, etc., all of which terms are often used interchangeably.

Shelf reading. The process of checking that library materials are arranged on the shelf according to classification number order. Performed on a recurring schedule, this ensures that materials are correctly filed.

Shelflist. A file arranged by call number identifying each title and every copy held by the library. The authoritative inventory listing of all classified materials within the library.

Software. The components, consisting of programs, that run computers and/or media operations.

Standing order. An order to a publisher or vendor to continue supplying a needed item until told to stop. Also known as "till forbidden" order.

Surrogates.   Data elements in bibliographic databases representing the original documents being analyzed. Common document surrogates include bibliographic citations, subject headings, and, in some cases, abstracts.

Telecommunications.   Use of voice grade and dedicated telephone lines as well as microwave stations to access remote databases via the computer terminal. Several third-party providers of networks have local telephone connections in most major and medium-sized cities. This local connection eliminates long-distance charges from any fees charged for network use.

Telefacsimile.   The process of sending exact duplicates of original documents to a remote site by means of an electronic telefacsimile machine and voice grade telephone lines.

Thesaurus.   A word list in alphabetic or classified order indicating the hierarchical relationships between terms. Indicates broader, narrower, and synonymous relationships between subject headings or descriptors.

Tickler file.   Used in library acquisitions for standing orders to remind the librarian that a desired work should be available and, if not yet received, that a follow-up should be initiated.

Upgrades.   Computer application programs including those for integrated library systems must continue to meet changing library needs. These enhancements or upgrades enable the library to stay current with improved technology.

User group.   The combined individuals the library hopes to serve.

Vendor.   A middleman between publishers and the library who supplies materials for library orders or approval plans. A convenient and effective means of eliminating excessive paperwork.

Weeding.   The process whereby librarians examine and remove materials no longer needed in the collection due to content, age, condition, or space requirements.

Index

About the Author

Robert A. Berk is chairman and professor of the Department of Information and Communication Sciences, and director of the Medical Library, School of Medicine at Southern Illinois University.